The Art of Knowing

The Art
of Knowing

The Poetry and Prose of

Conrad Aiken

Harry Marten

University of Missouri Press
Columbia, 1988

Copyright © 1988 by
The Curators of the University of Missouri
University of Missouri Press, Columbia, Missouri 65211
Printed and bound in the United States of America

Library of Congress Cataloging-in-Publication Data
Marten, Harry.

   The art of knowing: the poetry and prose of Conrad Aiken / Harry
Marten.
   p. cm.
Includes index.
ISBN 0-8262-0654-9
   1. Aiken, Conrad, 1889-1973—Criticism and interpretation.
I. Title.
PS3501.I5Z748   1988
818'.5209—dc19

For permission, see page 193.

To Ginit

Acknowledgments

Portions of chapters six and eleven were originally published in *ELH, Journal of Narrative Technique,* and *Studies in the Literary Imagination.* I am grateful to the editors of these journals for permission to use material from these articles.

This study was begun during my appointment as a Huntington Library Fellow, written in part during my year as an American Council of Learned Societies Fellow, and completed with the aid of the Humanities Faculty Development Fund of Union College. I am grateful for all of this support, and for grants from the Union College Library. The staffs of the Huntington Library, the Union College Library, and the Washington University Libraries have been unfailingly efficient and helpful. Daniel Woodward of the Huntington Library, Holly Hall of Washington University, and David Gerhan of Union College were especially considerate and helpful.

I am indebted to Mary H. Aiken for her hospitality, help, and encouragement, for permission to quote from Conrad Aiken's published and unpublished work, and for a photograph of Conrad Aiken; to Professor Joseph Killorin for assistance in selecting a photograph of Conrad Aiken; to Mrs. Robert J. Bender for permission to use her painting, by Mary H. Aiken, of Conrad Aiken in his Jeake's House study; to Florence and Fraser Bonnell for generously permitting me access to manuscript copy of their splendid *Conrad Aiken: A Bibliography;* to Thora Girke, a secretary without peer, for her careful and thoughtful work in preparing various drafts of the manuscript. My friend and colleague William M. Murphy has my special thanks for wise counsel, encouragement, and support. I owe Wayne Fields, Jim McCord, and Brenda Wineapple more than they can know. Their humor, honesty, and thoughtfulness have been examples for me. My deepest debts are to my parents, Abraham and Ann Marten, to my sons, Peter and Timothy, and especially to my wife, Ginit.

H. M.
July 1987

Contents

Texts and Abbreviations

When practical, notes referring to Conrad Aiken's works will be given parenthetically in the text. For the reader's convenience, I quote when possible from the readily available 1982 edition of *Selected Poems*. I have not regularized the spelling or punctuation of unpublished material. Ellipsis points used by Aiken in his original texts are indicated by unspaced ellipsis dots. My own omissions from these texts are indicated by regular spaced ellipsis points. I use the following abbreviations:

Texts by Aiken

BV, C, GC, HFG, KC: *Blue Voyage, Conversation, Great Circle, A Heart for the Gods of Mexico, King Coffin,* in *The Collected Novels of Conrad Aiken* (New York, Chicago, San Francisco: Holt, Rinehart and Winston, 1964)

CC: *Collected Criticism* (London, Oxford, New York: Oxford University Press, 1968)

CP: *Collected Poems,* 2d ed. (New York: Oxford University Press, 1970)

HEH: Conrad Aiken Collection, Henry E. Huntington Library, San Marino, California

SL: *Selected Letters of Conrad Aiken,* ed. Joseph Killorin (New Haven and London: Yale University Press, 1978)

SP: *Selected Poems* (New York: Schocken Books, 1982)

U: *Ushant* (New York: Oxford University Press, 1971)

WU: Conrad Aiken–Robert Linscott Letters, Conrad Aiken Papers, Special Collections, Washington University Libraries, St. Louis, Missouri

Interviews with Aiken

BBC I, BBC II: *Conversation with Conrad Aiken.* BBC Third

Programme. Two programs recorded in New York by D. G.
   Bridson, 11 January 1962 and 18 January 1962 (HEH).
Phoenix: "Please Continue Mr. Aiken," *Phoenix* (1966), 18- 29.
PR: "The Art of Poetry IX, Conrad Aiken: An Interview," *Paris
   Review* 42 (Spring 1968): 97-124.
Shenandoah: "An Interview with Conrad Aiken," *Shenandoah* 15
   (Autumn 1963): 18-40.

Life and living is

The effort to grasp

And be grasped,

To see,

And be seen,

To comprehend

And to be comprehended,

To know the other

And to be known

Conrad Aiken, "Knowing," ca. 1965,
Henry E. Huntington Library

1 Introduction
The Battle Joined

In 1940, with America at the brink of war, Conrad Aiken delivered his own declaration of battle—for the spirit and the intellectual energy of his art. It is a statement of aggression no critic of Aiken's work can ignore. In the August *Atlantic* he wrote of

> that sort of decay in taste which accompanies a decline in poetic energies, and which then organizes itself in defense, quite naturally, of the lesser and more arid virtues of poetry: the jejune precisions of artifice and formalism, the snug enclosures of wit and irony. (CC, 101)

A consistently careful craftsman himself,[1] Aiken observed the "withering of the poet's function" (CC, 102) and called for poets to

> throw the critics and schoolmasters out of the window, neck and crop, and the sociologists as well; and then themselves reëstablish poetry where it belongs—not in the margins of a textbook, but as coterminous with our awareness of the world. (CC, 102)

Aiken's prescription compels all but the most self-consumed critic to consider the nature of his own craft and intention. Recognizing honestly, with Aiken, that as critics we will "perceive those things to which we are attuned; and no matter . . . how fine we spin a logic in defense of our tastes . . . we subtilize the net of our temperament, the snare of our imperious desires, from which we are never destined to escape" (CC, 31), we nonetheless do well to realize with him too that "a critic qualifies as intelligent more by his awareness of aesthetic problems than by his solution of them" (CC, 74). This is especially so in studying a writer whose

1

subject from first to last was the seemingly inexhaustible variety
of ways one can know the world.

Poetry is "the highest speech of man," Aiken once declared. "It
will absorb and transmute . . . all that we can know. This has
always been, and always will be, poetry's office" (PR, 120).

What we want from [the poet] is intensity, both in the analytical and
*aff*ective parts of language; a complete honesty in seeing life as a
kaleidoscopic series of incandescent instants—sometimes apparently
meaningless, sometimes profound; that he . . . should have tasted truth
in all its inconsistencies of form. (CC, 82)[2]

If poetry is an art of changes that seeks, as Aiken suggests, to
"embody the full consciousness of man" (CC, 80), then the
critic's task must be to absorb, comprehend, and articulate the
series of shifting shapes and symbols. He must present "the
effects of contrasting and conflicting tones and themes, a kind of
underlying simultaneity and dissimilarity" (CC, 128), without
making a virtue of the pursuit of uniqueness, and yet without
taking recourse in doctrinaire formulae in order to render the
work universally intelligible. The critic must enable the reader to
see the particularity of the poem he reads as well as enable him to
see the sign of the poet on all his art.

In Aiken's case the "sign" was an attraction to order and historical resonance, as well as a fascination with the energies of the
new and free-formed. As a young American travelling to Europe
in 1911, Aiken looked for "vital contact with the historical sense"
(U, 22), keeping firmly to "his own slightly conservative bias, in
the persistent belief that form must be form, that inventions of
form must keep a basis in order and tradition" (U, 219). Drawn to
the England of his ancestors, with its "finished forms and rituals
of a fixed and conscious society of fine lives in fine houses, in a
social frame that was . . . finely elaborate" (U, 303), Aiken experienced "the shadow of the Old Country falling with a disturbing
and revealing suggestiveness on the simple planes of the new" (U,
135). Yet as an American often turning homeward again, he rel-
ished the "new civilization," (U, 137) which was

still in the process of formation, of evolution: a new language . . . this minute in its most fascinating stage, the stage of concrescence and emergence: you could feel it on every side of you . . . the inexhaustible inventiveness. . . . Could one find in England any comparable fecundity? . . . And could it turn out to be anything less than suicidal, spiritually and morally, if one were to abandon this for the outworn refinements, the tarnished subtleties and snobbisms, of a society which was visibly dying on its feet, and from which one's ancestors had come away precisely for that reason? (U, 137)

In many ways a traditional writer, then, Aiken was nonetheless a connoisseur of chaos. And though it may frustrate a reader's penchant for resolution, an evaluation of Aiken's work must be one that explores mixed modes and meanings, recognizing energies as much as patterns.

What Aiken once called a "principle of uprootedness" (U, 20) lies at the heart of his lifelong restlessness, his fascination with ambiguity, and his perpetual effort both to affirm and deny flux and fragmentation. Its foundation surely was laid on the terrible February morning in 1901 when Aiken, age eleven, woke to hear voices raised in argument, then shots, and discovered his parents dead in their bedroom: "I had to step over my father's body to go to my mother. But she was dead, her mouth wide open in the act of screaming. . . . Then I walked to the police station a block away and told them my father had shot my mother and himself" (SL, 4). "Finding them dead," Aiken recalled a half-century later, he "found himself possessed of them forever" (U, 302) yet also dispossessed, in a stunning moment, of home and family and all familiar places, as his fictionalized account in *Blue Voyage* suggests:

... she still looked alive but extraordinarily still. . . . "Yes, William, I am dead. But I know you are there. . . . A dreadful accident has occurred. . . . Run and wake Nanny. Shut the door into the nursery. Wind the clocks on Sunday morning. And say good-bye to this house and world forever. (BV, 100)

Taken from the warmth of Savannah and plunged into the physical and emotional chill of New England, Aiken was separated from his brothers, Kemp and Rob, and his sister, Elizabeth, who were adopted by the wealthy efficiency expert Frederick Winslow Taylor, while Aiken was, as he describes it, "bandied about from one relative to another, from aunt to uncle to cousin, for a decade therefore more at home in school or college than in any corner of any house" (U, 73-74). He "had become for the entire family an embarrassing symbol, a reminder, the something that had been sacrificed" (U, 74).

"But what were we to do, what could have been done—? Where was the money to come from, who was to look after you? how take care of three orphaned children with not a penny anywhere to be seen? You can see how it was. A decision had to be made, and quickly. And then came Cousin Ted's offer to take Wide and Handsome, which was all very well for them, but had the effect of leaving *you* out in the cold—financially, socially, psychologically, totally. They vanished out of your life, and you out of theirs; behind those giant box hedges, they were to all intents imprisoned from you; they ascended into a world of grandeur which by its very splendor and munificence was only to increase your feeling of isolation." (U, 75-76)

Neither the Middlesex School in Concord—which he attended for years and where, as he said later, "the Emerson-Thoreau-Hawthorne thing went into [his] gizzard" (Shenandoah, 22)—nor Harvard—where he studied with George Santayana, discovered his vocation, and got to know T. S. Eliot—offered the displaced young man a genuine place of his own. The man who grew out of this time of trauma and rejection was to spend a lifetime composing a "moving pattern of meaning and design out of which he was . . . all the while directing his confused and changing aim or aims" (U, 103). Even as "the sense of one's separateness as an individual" demanded "its own necessary expansions and discoveries" (U, 49), and as the poet sought to uncover "the component materials of evolving attitudes" (U, 103) that would enable him to take possession of his private worlds, he was to discover that

one of the effects of having been orphaned, and further orphaned by the adoption of R. and K. by Cousin Ted . . . [was] quite simply the need of, and search for, a home . . . a sustaining, but above all *uninstitutional, locus of one's own.* (U, 72)

Convinced that "to be able to *separate* oneself from one's background, one's environment" was "the most thrilling discovery of which consciousness was capable" (U, 32), Aiken nonetheless, perhaps of necessity, sought "a point of rest, one to which he could return with every confidence of safety and enrichment" (U, 78). He found finally not one, but three "homes": Jeake's House in Rye, England; the house he named "41 Doors" in Brewster on Cape Cod; and, for part of each of his last twelve years, 230 Oglethorpe Avenue in Savannah, next door to the house where he had lived his first eleven years. "England . . . had been a window . . . which it had been his imperative need to find and to open: the window which looked upon his own racial and cultural past, and thus bestowed upon him the sense of belonging, of being part of . . . the evolving series of civilized consciousness" (U, 279); New England offered "a dynamic . . . potential" (U, 217), combining a strong sense of family history and literary inheritance with the energy of a still comparatively new land and language; and the city of Savannah provided the opportunity for an "all-healing recapitulation, this triumph of repossession" in the poet's old age, "flooding his veins and arteries with recollected beauty and power" (U, 339). Aiken's secure and sometimes simultaneous identification with all three places, mingling—sometimes colliding—with his obsessive pursuit of new places of land and mind, shaped and reshaped his writing, and therefore his identity, throughout his career. For as Aiken explained in *Ushant,* his "nature" had to "learn to shape itself in words; words and the rhythms of words, were the medium in which it seemed most likely, or at any rate most happily and magically, to find the equivalents of being, the equivalents of the . . . shadowy self" (U, 92).

The "words" of "Senlin: A Biography," which we will study in chapter 2, were published in 1918, when Aiken was living in Boston. He had finished at Harvard, had married Jessie McDonald, had become a father to a son and daughter, had lived for a time in England (where he had introduced typescripts of Eliot's "Prufrock" and "La Figlia Che Piange" to generally skeptical readers and to the instantly enthusiastic Ezra Pound), and had launched his own writing career with *Earth Triumphant and Other Tales in Verse* (1914), *Turns and Movies and Other Tales in Verse* (1916), *The Jig of Forslin* (1916), and *Nocturne of Remembered Spring and Other Poems* (1917). In many ways "Senlin" is the center of the series of loosely narrative poetic "symphonies" that compose Aiken's major early work, *The Divine Pilgrim* ("The Charnel Rose," written in 1915; "The Jig of Forslin," 1915-1916; "The House of Dust," 1916-1917; "Senlin," 1918; "The Pilgrimage of Festus," 1919-1920; and "Changing Mind," written in 1925 and added later as a kind of coda). These are poems where meaning "will not be found in the particular phrase or line . . . but rather, as is true of music, in the totality of emotional and sensory effect, the balancing of episode and episode, mood and mood, overtone and overtone" (SL, 38). As Aiken described it, "Senlin" is

an extension and analysis of that perennially fascinating problem of personal identity which perplexes each of us all his life: the basic and possibly unanswerable question, *who and what am I?* . . . Unanswerable except perhaps in a kind of serial dishevelment of answers, or partial answers. . . . Senlin may be taken as the generic "I" of the series of poems that compose *The Divine Pilgrim,* the unit of human reference upon which it rests. (CP, 1022)

A poem that considers the nature of the human psyche, exploring relationships between haunting urban landscapes and mindscapes, "Senlin" is most importantly a poem that crystallizes Aiken's early efforts to experiment with ideas of perception and reality.

In the fall of 1921, shortly after the publication in February of *Punch: The Immortal Liar, Documents in His History,* Aiken moved his family to England, settling in Lookout Cottage, Winchelsea, Sussex, then settling, in 1924, in Jeake's House, Rye, Sussex—"the beautiful house" (U, 250) where he was to do much

of his best work. "Punch" extends Aiken's fascination with possibilities of knowing, offering an elaborate puppet show of creative modes and methods. The reader is challenged to rethink the
idea of poetic fictions, mimetic realities and illusions, literary
forms and sensibilities from farce to grotesque. Composed soon
after, "John Deth: A Metaphysical Legend" (1930, first versions
1922-1924) mixes myth, the grotesque, the macabre, caricature,
philosophy, and psychosexuality even more explicitly and com-
plexly to expand Aiken's vision of the stages of human consciousness.

"Changing Mind" (1930, written 1925), Aiken's intensely interior poem "built on a series of dreams, with simply the notion of
portraying the mind in a moment of affective transition" (SL,
167), and "The Coming Forth by Day of Osiris Jones" (1931), "a
behaviorist drama" in which "everything, almost, is reported scientifically and in brief notes from outside" (SL, 171), are explored
side by side in this study. Together they provide a frame around
fifteen years of concentrated creative activity in which "the relation 'I: World'" (CC, 98)—the relationship between subjective
and objective perceptions and the ways in which a poet can render them—was Aiken's subject.

Aiken once described his stay in England as "the wonderful
decade or more. . . . A time of blooming, of profusion, of hard
work and endless debate; of good food, good drinks and good
living" (U, 232). It was a time too "of competitive stress" (U, 232)
and sometimes of "the most fearful—really terrifying—state of
poverty" (WU, 12 March 1925) he had ever known. Despite
receiving the Pulitzer Prize for his *Selected Poems* (1929), he was
compelled to write to his brother as late as July 1932 that

I've got . . . a whole book of short stories on hand which I haven't been
able to sell; and at least three of them as good stories as I ever wrote. . . .
To work without either response or reward can't go on forever. . . . It
isn't as if I were a useless creature, either, or as if I weren't doing something. I've worked damned hard in the last two years: an output of three
books of verse, one of short stories, and two thirds of a novel, in that
period, is nothing to be ashamed of, especially as I believe it to be my
best work. (SL, 189-90)

Throughout this period Aiken endured personal upheavals as well: the dissolution of his marriage to Jessie, his wedding to Clarissa Lorenz in 1930, his marriage to Mary Hoover in 1937, his displacement from Jeake's House during the change of relationships, and his subsequent returns to the house as a renter. Yet Aiken's creative energy continued unabated. Never quite comfortable as a novelist, Aiken nonetheless published five novels between 1927 and 1940. The first three, especially, clarify and extend his exploration of the ways the individual and the world and "the conscious and the unconscious were engaged, had always been engaged, in a dance, the most intricate and surprising and involved and contrapuntal of dances" (U, 243) of mutual definition. Each of these works of fiction suggests aspects of seeing the human consciousness "in action," from the essentially poetic and relatively plotless *Blue Voyage* (1927), a tale of one man's ocean crossing from America to England which offers a "kind of singular abstraction and attenuated contact with the real, an 'absoluteness'" (CC, 167), to *Great Circle* (1933), an obviously autobiographical tale which centers on a memory of a parental murder-suicide and which Aiken defined as "psychoanalytic in form" (WU, 1 June 1931), to *King Coffin* (1935), a more traditionally plotted story of desocialization, violence, and suicide. These mimetic tales offer a suggestive complement to the explorations of kinds of knowing prevalent in the more abstract lyrics of the period.

In the late 1920s through the mid-1930s Aiken intermittently wrote "Preludes for Memnon" (1931) and "Time in the Rock" (1936), the 159 lyrics of his "serial essays . . . on attitude and definition . . . *nuclei* of awareness and self-awareness" (U, 320). Together with the long creation-myth "Landscape West of Eden" (1934), they represent an effort to crystallize his philosophic and psychological attitudes. These works are, Aiken told an interviewer, "in the nature of precepts . . . and are also at the same time an approach to a kind of religion without dogma" (BBC II, 7). More meditative and analytical than his earlier verses, less playful with words and perceptual possibilities, these poems stand at the center of his life's work, "providing a greater height from which to see things, and a greater space in which to spread them" (BBC II, 2).

Moved as always by a "dualism that profoundly suited him" (U, 134), Aiken found himself in the late 1930s strongly drawn back to "so much in America that was still virginal and tentative" (U, 134). Partly because of the beginnings of war in Europe, which compelled departure from England, partly because of the emptiness that seemed to follow the career-culminating achievement of the "Preludes," and no doubt partly because of the life he was beginning to build with Mary Hoover, his third wife, Aiken was ripe for change. In 1939, returning with mixed feelings to Cape Cod, where he could live more safely and cheaply, Aiken found that he could "enjoy the American scene whole heartedly again" (U, 135). The energy he discovered in finding an "'open sesame' . . . to a truer understanding" (U, 289) of his old-new country is reflected throughout his work: at first in somewhat tentative exploration of America as place and metaphor in his last two novels, *A Heart for the Gods of Mexico* (1939) and *Conversation: or Pilgrims' Progress* (1940), and then more emphatically in poems like "Mayflower" (1945), "The Kid" (1947), and "Hallowe'en" (1949), which merge his interests in American issues and their relationships to European forms with his continuing exploration of human perception and individual consciousness.

Aiken found himself claimed by his ancestral roots: "The ancestors, the ancestors, the unconquerable ancestors, whose tongues still spoke so clearly, whose hands still reached so unmistakably, and whose wills were so indistinguishable from one's own! . . . Each bud, and then each leaf, each flower, taking up the precious pattern, repeating it" (U, 45). Still, the process of reclaiming and being reclaimed by America and "his own ghosts in it" (U, 336) was a complex one. And "Mayflower," "The Kid," and "Hallowe'en" in particular, central poems of the period, involve more than one idea of ancestry and take the poet and reader down many paths of understanding of self and place through American myths and folktales, rhythms and rhymes, colloquial and formal dictions, public and private histories, personal and familial experiences and memories, individual and archetypal figures.

Aiken once worried that when "one felt at home, one would have no more to learn, or would . . . be no longer capable of learning" (U, 334). Secure at "41 Doors" in Brewster by the mid-1950s and having achieved both a clear literary and an intense personal response to American places and people, Aiken chose in "A Letter from Li Po" (1955) and "The Crystal" (1958), major poems of his late period, to affirm that being "home" need not mean complacency. Often speaking with a voice of exile, mingling and merging American scenes, characters, and voices with distant locales, historical figures, and legends, Aiken broadened the range of his final philosophic meditations. He discovered once again, in old age as he had throughout his long career, fresh ways to comprehend and represent "the 'precarious gait we call experience'" (U, 11).

This study does not attempt to present a thesis that answers Aiken's work. Neither is the study an effort, save incidentally, to "place" Aiken amidst his contemporaries or amidst currents of modern and postmodern literary criticism; nor is it an endeavor to offer an analysis of the self-acknowledged obvious influences upon his work, among them Melville, Henry and William James, Santayana, Freud, and Jung. Such concerns, while enlightening, direct the reader's attention away from the work itself—certainly the main concern if one is to rediscover and appreciate the immense variety, energy, and beauty of the writings of this probably least read of major modern American authors.

My text refers throughout to Aiken's own criticism and letters in order to clarify the poetry and prose fiction. References to and from Aiken's creative autobiography *Ushant* are threaded through the study in ways that I believe illuminate the texts being observed and reveal the complexity and distinctness of the autobiography itself. The study does not consider Aiken's short stories or the single play *(Mr. Arcularis)* that grew out of one of them. The thematic and technical concerns of these works of fiction are, I believe, more completely embodied in his ambitious novels and narrative poems. I seek here to offer neither encyclopedic attention to all of Aiken's work nor a rating of his best efforts. Rather I attempt to present readings of works that, representing Aiken's life with words, will illuminate his search to comprehend and express the possibilities of human knowing.

If I help readers discover or rediscover Conrad Aiken's creative intentions and achievements, opening ways of reading the inter-related poetry and fiction, I will have achieved my goal. To bring reader and writer together, free of the obfuscating rhetoric of critical theorizing or systematizing, is, I believe, the most uniquely satisfying function of criticism.

2 Mixed Modes and Methods

"Senlin" at the Center

O~n~ 6 September 1914, Macmillan brought out the tentative, too-mannered poems of Conrad Aiken's first collection: *Earth Triumphant and Other Tales in Verse.* By 1925, the year he recorded on the endpaper of his own copy of the poems that these were "Hopeless / Not to be reprinted / 'Except Innocence,'"[1] Aiken had written eight more volumes of poems, a book of critical essays, and one of short stories.[2] By 1930 Aiken was a Pulitzer Prize winner firmly launched on one of the richest careers in modern literary history. These first sixteen years of steady writing do not mark a straight line of poetic progress, however. There are uneven works amidst the excellent ones, lapses of taste and power amidst great strength. Many of the major poems are long narrative meditations and suffer the fate of most long poems, moving in valleys and peaks rather than with sustained intensity. Of course, as M. L. Rosenthal and Sally M. Gall have recently observed, "*A poem depends for its life neither on continuous narration nor on developed argument but on a progression of specific . . . intensities of emotionally and sensuously charged awareness.* A successful long poem, and the modern sequence pre-eminently, is made up of such centers of intensity."[3] And the unevenness of Aiken's work is itself an indicator of poetic intent. Aiken, a lifelong poet of changes, chose early and deliberately to use a variety of styles and voices, discovering and revealing himself in the process.

Almost twenty years before the publication of Aiken's first volume, W. B. Yeats had given ample evidence of a symbolist ascendancy in important English poetry. The French had already demonstrated that words can mean volumes without corresponding referentially to things. The task of poetry was not to inform but to evoke, not to name things but to create their atmosphere. Arthur Rimbaud in "Voyelles" made cosmic statements about the alphabet, indicating that associations of sounds with ideas and moods help readers to discover meaning.[4] And Paul Verlaine in "Chanson D'Automne" convinced his readers—with a gathering of weighty vowel sounds and a profusion of rhymes at intervals of no more than four syllables—that "violins of autumn," whatever they might be exactly, can "wound" a heart with "monotonous languor."[5]

Yeats, in the 1896 version of "He Remembers Forgotten Beauty"—even more so in that of 1899—took equally great pains to obscure poetic statement. Wrenching syntax to present a study in vagueness, he performed a ritual suggesting the poet's priestlike ability to transubstantiate the common while leaving uncertain the nature of the new object, thus the last lines in the 1896 version:

And when you sigh from kiss to kiss
I hear white Beauty sighing, too,
For hours when all must fade like dew,
Till there be naught but throne on throne
Of seraphs, brooding, each alone,
A sword upon his iron knees,
On her most lonely mysteries.

These become even vaguer in 1899:

I hear white Beauty sighing, too,
For hours when all must fade like dew,
But flame on flame, and deep on deep,
Throne over throne where in half sleep,
Their swords upon their iron knees,
Brood her high lonely mysteries.[6]

Aiken's own version of the symbolist impulse is crystallized beyond a doubt in the June 1919 self-review of *The Charnel Rose* for *Poetry* magazine. Calling for "a sort of absolute poetry," a procedure in which the poet is "not content to present emotions or things or sensations for their own sakes,"

this method takes only the most delicately evocative aspects of them, makes of them a keyboard, and plays upon them a music of which the chief characteristic is its elusiveness, its fleetingness, and its richness in the shimmering overtones of hint and suggestion. (CP, 1028)[7]

But the time of *Earth Triumphant* was also the time of "imagism," of Ezra Pound's and F. S. Flint's manifesto calling on poets to render "direct treatment of the 'thing,'" and to "use absolutely no word that did not contribute to the presentation."[8] And when Pound further defined the image in his 1914 *Gaudier-Brzeska* as ". . . a radiant node or cluster; . . . what I can, and must perforce, call a VORTEX, from which, and through which, and into which ideas are constantly rushing,"[9] serious poets listened. Though Aiken was soon to reject most of what, along with Pound, he called " Amy'gism" (PR, 107)—after Amy Lowell, one of the movement's founders and chief (perhaps only real) practitioner—portions of his poetry continued to show a hard attention to the ideas and emotions conveyed in a world of things.[10]

A full view of the first decades of Conrad Aiken's work suggests that from the beginning he was self-consciously a user of "isms" rather than a convert. His goal was to render neither the subjective nor the objective, but to consider and to call the reader's attention to the relationship of the perspectives. Seeking to know the comforts and the limits of form *and* the excitement and fluidity of pushing past received patterns, he presented to his readers a carefully chosen profusion of modes. As he wrote in the 1916 preface to *The Jig of Forslin:*

"The Jig of Forslin" . . . does not conveniently fit in any category, and is therefore liable, like all such works, to be condemned for not being something it was never intended to be. . . . For my intention has been to employ all methods, attitudes, slants, each in its proper place. . . .
    Cacophonies and irregularities have often been deliberately employed as contrast. Free rhythms, and rhymeless verse, have been used, also, to introduce variety of movement. Mood and movement, in general, have

been permitted to fluctuate together, as they would seem to do automatically if not violated by too arbitrary choice of pattern ... This does not mean, however, that there has been no choice of pattern whatever. (CP, 1018-19)

There are different patterns, variations, and explosions of patterns for different poems, of course, but in general Aiken's procedure was to focus on a series of subjective beings who in turn contemplate the outer reality of things. We see minds at work, the externals these beings perceive, the transformations by perceiver of thing perceived. At times, it is true, we see little more than objects; and at times, too, objective realities fracture into a multiplicity of dreamlike thoughts and motions, as we find it difficult to comprehend more than mindscape. Still, more often than not, what Aiken finally gives us is a complex coherence in which, as Georges Poulet has written of Gustave Flaubert, things "are constantly fused together in the unity of a single perceptive mind," whereas that mind "is kept from disappearing in the flux of its own consciousness by the objectivity of a world with which it is in constant touch."[11]

Let us consider locations and dislocations, using as an example "Senlin: A Biography," a central poem of the period. Aiken tells us in the first line of his 1918 poetic symphony, "Senlin sits before us, and we see him" (SP, 12).[12] With such a sharp declarative statement in front of him, the reader settles in comfortably to await the obvious who-what-when-and-where of the start of a familiar Browningesque drama.[13] And biography, after all, is nothing if not the act of organizing and rendering the "facts" of a life for all to see. "He smokes his pipe before us, and we hear him" (SP, 12). Better and better: not only are we about to discover what the man looks like and where he is, but we are also about to find out, in his own words, what is on his mind. What follows, however, is not information, not even speculation. Rather it is a series of questions—still pertaining to the nature of the "objective" things being laid out before us, but making us wonder where we are, where we are headed, and with a kind of subliminal recollection of the certainty that is fast fading, why we ever thought we were being located in space and time in the first place.

Is he small, with reddish hair,
Does he light his pipe with a meditative stare,
And a pointed flame reflected in both eyes?
Is he sad and happy and foolish and wise?
Did no one see him enter the doors of the city,
Looking about him at roofs and trees and skies?

(SP, 12)

At least we still have a "city," with buildings, greenery, and open spaces beyond; and finally the promised "voice" comes forth to answer our many questions. But when the man of many turns, if indeed man he be, speaks at last, we discover that the promise of specificity was a kind of conjuror's trick. Aiken is doing what myth-making word-magicians have been doing for millennia: tying a knot that intertwines space and time—rendering the once-upon-a-time of a mythic hero.[14] Even this insight, though, turns out to be too simple a comprehension, as metamorphoses continue, always with the hint (merely that, but clearly) that the reader, the author, and the character are someplace possible to measure, locate, and search out with the senses. Aiken is careful not to let his readers complacently replace the broken promise of a real world with a different category of perception that contains its own distinct and systematic counternorms. The confusions of "Senlin" do not resolve themselves if we substitute the conventions of myth, fable, or fairy tale for those of reality.

The familiar is continually made unfamiliar, in the object world and in the presentation of various recognizable literary structures, as modes of seeing collide and jostle one another. The reader—who is given no firm vantage point and who is made to recognize, but mistrust or feel uncomfortable with, the shifting modes of presentation and perception—discovers not so much a systematic completeness as the complexities of the act of knowing. "I stepped from a cloud," Senlin says, "as evening fell" (SP, 12); it is a fine, mythlike thing for our pipe smoker to do. But there are variations:

"I walked on the sound of a bell;
I ran with winged heels along a gust;

Or is it true that I laughed and sprang from dust? ...
. . . .
Has no one, on a mountain in the spring,
Heard Senlin sing?
Perhaps I came alone on a snow-white horse,—
Riding alone from the deep-starred night.
Perhaps I came on a ship whose sails were music,—
Sailing from moon or sun on a river of light."

He lights his pipe with a pointed flame.

(SP, 12)

It is almost as if Senlin—or Aiken—were rehearsing for us the ways in which a story can be told. And yet this is more serious than simply a poem-about-poetry summary of the aesthetics of storytelling openings. For Senlin is not just a narrator thinking of ways to begin; he *is* his various beginnings—all of them. Senlin is the creating consciousness, and his mysteries of definition mark the very terrain we inhabit as readers who perceive and, in perceiving, half create both natural and literary places.

Has Senlin become a forest? Do we walk in Senlin?
Is Senlin the wood we walk in,—ourselves,—the world?
Senlin! we cry ... Senlin! again ... No answer,
Only soft broken echoes backward whirled ...

Yet we would say: this is no wood at all,
But a small white room with a lamp upon the wall;
And Senlin, before us, pale, with reddish hair,
Lights his pipe with a meditative stare.

(SP, 13)

When we consider Senlin, we risk becoming lost in him. Yet we have been pulled away from such immersion as the poem's first section concludes. We have come full circle, back to some sort of natural world—with Senlin just another inhabitant rather than a realm of multiple possibilities himself. We have come back, however, both enlarged and confused by our sense of other, often larger or more complex—sometimes simply more literarily artificial—realities. Then, even as we are being made to recognize the boundaries of our imaginings, signposts of space and place once again dissolve into elemental forms that, acted upon by both the creating and the reasoning imagination, refuse to be still. We realize, "The city dissolves about us; and its walls / Are mountains of rock cruelly carved by wind" (SP, 13).

Yet we would say: there are no rocks at all
Nor desert of sand … here by a city wall
White lights jewel the evening, black roots freeze,
And Senlin turns his head to look at trees.

(SP, 14)

Senlin: the name is repeated with certainty as if in the performance of some temporal ritual that will establish a still point in a turning world but that will not itself stop the world's spin. What "Senlin says" leads us into and out of the chaos of rational and irrational, literary and naturalistic worlds intertwined. "It is evening, Senlin says. . . . It is morning. . . . It is noontime. . . . It is moonlight" (SP, 14, 21, 26, 33), as the poem seems to yoke us to some sense of progress through a natural, irrevocable cycle. But much of the "cycle" is now most noticeably literary, rather than natural. At evening we enter into a Keatsian or Shelleyan cosmos[15] where at "lilac dusk" mysterious "White unicorns come gravely down to the water" (SP, 14), and

Stars hang over the purple waveless sea;
A sea on which no sail was ever lifted,
Where a human voice was never heard.
The shadows of vague hills are dark on the water,
The silent stars seem silently to sing.

(SP, 14)

And in the clear light of noontime, when tradition tells us that reason dominates perceptions—with "the sunshine a harsh chord" (SP, 26) and with Senlin's soul stretching out before us like "a city / With noisily peopled streets" (SP, 16)—we seem invited to perceive the inner and outer scenes as if entering into the beginnings of an episode of naturalistic fiction. We recall the literary territory Aiken already explored a year or so earlier in "The House of Dust," a symphonic poem about the city and the "crowd-man" (CP, 1020) inhabiting it.

Cold rain lashes the car-roof, scurries in gusts,
Streams down the windows in waves and ripples of lustre;
The lamps in the streets are distorted and strange.
Someone takes his watch from his pocket and yawns.
One peers out in the night for the place to change.
                                    (CP, 123)

And we remember the even earlier urban melodrama of "The Jig of Forslin":

The walls of the city are rolled away;
And suddenly all the lighted rooms are bare,
Numberless gas-jets flare,
Thousands of secret lives, with unconcern,
Yawn and turn.
Men in their shirtsleeves reading papers,
Women by mirrors, combing out their hair,
Children sleeping, old men dying,
. . . .
Wheels rumble, the men rush out of bars
To see great horses pass.
Thick flames burst from the windows and spout up walls,
The firemen's faces are white in the ghastly light. . . .
                                    (CP, 112, 113)

But in "Senlin" we soon move from primary awareness of shifting literary constructions to psychological perceptions. As we follow the dizzying music of "a street piano" (SP, 26) the "sharp notes flash and dazzle and turn," becoming "Memory's knives."

They ripple and lazily burn.
. . . .

And I, in a horror of sunlight, stand alone.
                                    (SP, 26)

The suggestions of the real, albeit impressionistic, give way to the shadowy landscape of the surreal:

Do not recall my weakness, savage music!
Let the knives rest!
Impersonal, harsh, the music revolves and glitters,
And the notes like poniards pierce my breast.
And I remember the shadows of webs on stones,
And the sound of rain on withered grass,
And a sorrowful face that looked without illusions
At its image in the glass.

Do not recall my childhood, pitiless music!
The green blades flicker and gleam. . . .
                                    (SP, 26)

   The juxtapositions of image fragments, rough and wounding, with the more abstract but still unsettling sounds and pictures, and with the softer music that sets a basic rhythm throughout the poem, further disturb us:

Senlin, walking beside us, swings his arms. . . .
. . . .
"Did I, then, stretch from the bitter earth like these ? . . ."
. . . .
(Immense and solitary in a desert of rocks
Behold a bewildered oak
With white clouds screaming through its leafy brain.)
                                    (SP, 13)

   We are discovering nothing less than the nature of human understanding. As Santayana has said:

Our logical thoughts dominate experience only as the parallels and meridians make a checkerboard of the sea. They guide our voyage without controlling the waves, which toss for ever in spite of our ability to ride over them to our chosen ends. . . .

Out of the neglected riches of this dream the poet fetches his wares. He dips into the chaos that underlies the rational shell of the world and brings up some superfluous image, some emotion dropped by the way, and reattaches it to the present object . . . [and] he paints in again into the landscape the tints which the intellect has allowed to fade from it. If he seems sometimes to obscure a fact, it is only because he is restoring an experience.[16]

Senlin, then, a jumble of logical and illogical images and emotions, is "a house . . . locked and darkened, / Sealed from the sun with wall and door and blind" (SP, 20). He is "a city ... In the blue light of evening / Wind wanders among [his] streets" (SP, 21). He is a "room of rock" or "a door" before which darkness roils.

Knock on the door,—and you shall have an answer.
Open the heavy walls to set me free,
And blow a horn to call me into the sunlight,—
And startled, then, what a strange thing you shall see!
Nuns, murderers, and drunkards, saints and sinners,
Lover and dancing girl and sage and clown
Will laugh upon you, and you will find me nowhere.
I am a room, a house, a street, a town.
                                        (SP, 21)

As we strain for stability amidst the carefully controlled constructions and deconstructions of physical, psychological, and aesthetic landscapes, we are learning, quite literally, a paradoxical message as old in literature as Blake, Wordsworth, and Emerson. There is, Aiken tells us, a separateness and a reciprocity in the nature of things without which we could not exist. We cannot build any structures (houses, rooms, city streets) that will not by their very nature enclose as well as push back formlessness. We cannot expect complete order, or tolerate complete disorder; we must not neatly separate the beautiful from the ugly, the pleasing from the painful; we cannot tell in any permanent way subject from object, giver from taker, doer from recipient, one place from another. Nor can we fail to recognize the distinctness of the parts that make up the whole of our seeing. We can only continue to try to comprehend and accept the contraries as they collide, the diversity as it appears and disappears, and our own inevitable search for configuration *and* for freedom from binding form.

"A painter told me," Ralph Waldo Emerson wrote, "that nobody could draw a tree without in some sort becoming a tree."[17] This might be equally said of the poet, personae, or reader who discovers and reveals in "Senlin" the Emersonian "condition of true naming on the poet's part."[18]

"You will think it strange," says Senlin, "but this tree
Utters profound things . . .
And in its silence speaks to me.
I have sensations, when I stand beneath it,
As if its leaves looked at me. . . .

. . . .

'Regard,' they seem to say,
'Our idiot root, which going its brutal way
Has cracked your garden wall!
Ugly, is it not?
A desecration of this place ...
And yet, without it, could we exist at all?'

. . . .

Sometimes it seems as if there grew
In the dull garden of my mind
A tree like this, which, singing with delicate leaves,
Yet cracks the walls with cruel roots and blind.
Sometimes, indeed, it appears to me
That I myself am such a tree ..."

... And as we hear from Senlin these strange words
So, slowly, in the sunlight, he becomes this tree.
                                        (SP, 16-17)

As it began, "Senlin" ends, with an unsettling clash of certainty and change, more questions than solutions.

Senlin alone before us, played a music.
Was it himself he played? . . .

. . . .
"Walk on a hill and call me: 'Senlin! ... Senlin! ...'
Will I not answer you as clearly as now?
Listen to rain, and you will hear me speaking.
Look for my heart in the breaking of a bough ..."

Senlin stood before us in the sunlight,
And laughed, and walked away.
Did no one see him leaving the doors of the city,
Looking behind him as if he wished to stay?
Has no one, in the forests of the evening,
Heard the sad horn of Senlin slowly blown?
For somewhere, in the worlds-in-worlds about us,
He changes still, unfriended and alone.

(SP, 35-36)

By the time we finish "Senlin," Aiken has drawn for us a picture whose contours—now precise, now hazy, ever shifting—provide superb clues of how we may best grasp the whole of his early work. If we are not to get lost as we move through his poetic domain, we must continually interpret the terrain for ourselves. For now, the idea of constant change seems to explain Aiken's ideal of form.

3 Puppets and Showmanship
"Punch: The Immortal Liar"

With "Senlin" and its fellow "symphonies" of *The Divine Pilgrim* series at the philosophic center of Aiken's early work, Aiken's poems of the 1920s continued to experiment with the poet's and the reader's perception of the shapes and textures of reality. Recognizing "Senlin" as "the generic 'I' . . . the unit of human reference" (CP, 1022) upon which the series rests, we have discovered implicit in the series "the theory that was to underlie much of the later work" (CP, 1021),

namely, that in the evolution of man's consciousness, ever widening and deepening and subtilizing his awareness, and in his dedication of himself to this supreme task, man possesses all that he could possibly require in the way of a religious credo: when the half-gods go, the gods arrive. (CP, 1021)

In the 1930s Aiken would present—in what is probably his most important poetry—a sequence of well-considered, though not rigidly binding, aesthetic and intellectual formulations: preludes to attitude and preludes to definition.[1] But in the years just before, he was still discovering and exploring with dazzling dexterity and variety the possibilities of his art and its relationship (mimetic and otherwise) to life. Among other things added to his experimental terrain were a cosmic, sometimes comic, Punch and Judy show (*Punch: The Immortal Liar, Documents in His History*, 1921) and an extravagant "Metaphysical Legend" (*John Deth: A Metaphysical Legend, and Other Poems*, 1930, early version, 1922-1924). He composed a coda to his symphony series, mixing unusually intense and terrifying dreamscapes and psy-

chological analysis with vaudevillian antics and journalese
("Changing Mind," 1925); and he fashioned a kind of stenographic behaviorist drama that compels the reader to grasp the
strange aesthetic mixing of such diverse imaginative sources as
The Egyptian Book of the Dead and a medical student's daily
record book (*The Coming Forth by Day of Osiris Jones*, 1931).

First consider "Punch," a drama of puppets, puppeteers, and
illusions. On 3 December 1921, Aiken wrote from London to his
friend and sometime informal literary agent Robert Linscott:

> "Punch," meanwhile, is sharing the ostracism of his author. It's been out
> over a month, with no sale and no reviews, save a tiny "note" in the
> *Times* which appeared day before yesterday. Other papers haven't even
> listed it as among books received. And the *Times* note observes that it's
> mostly in *rhymed decasyllabics* (there's not one in the book). . . . Why
> on earth did I come here to begin all over again this abominable and
> hopeless struggle for *some* sort of recognition! What an idiot I am, what
> a preposterous biped wearing spectacles and an air of melancholy, a
> walking lamentation, a grief clad in a union-suit. (SL, 63)

The American edition had in fact been enthusiastically reviewed
by Amy Lowell in the 28 September 1921 *New Republic*. Lowell
had high praise for Aiken: "The drama of the man Punch
becomes the tragedy of blind, yearning, cheated humanity. The
poet rises to his climax inevitably and with a high seriousness."[2]
But perhaps her remarks point directly to the problems of recep-
tion the new work was having. Punch, quite simply, is not a
"man." Whatever else he may be in Aiken's unusual show, he is a
puppet with a long theatrical tradition that we must bring to the
poem or else the title and much of the action make no sense. And
his is not a tradition of "high seriousness." Of course in this poem
Punch is also Aiken's enigma: both creator and thing created. He
may well be an embodiment of some "tragedy of . . . yearning
. . . humanity," but a reader must get through many layers of dis-
guises, sexual innuendos, farce, and gothicism before he can
accept that comfortable literary formulation. "Punch" must have
been discomforting for its first readers, as it is both difficult and
rewarding for us now, because it invites application of a number

of literary and extra-literary touchstones simultaneously. It is not simply realistic or surrealistic, high-toned or low, introspective or extroverted. It offers, in fact, not one focus of perception but several, which are not to be blended one into the other. It is Aiken's experiment on the nature of fictions and their makers.

Almost a century before Aiken wrote "Punch," Charles Dickens, the master fiction maker–puppeteer, presented his readers with a still useful perspective on this matter of fictions. In the world of *The Old Curiosity Shop,* inhabited by weak-legged giants and wrinkled dwarves, men on stilts and dancing dogs, we find quite suddenly a still point. For a moment one of the shows within the show of the whole novel is at an end; we discover "Punch utterly devoid of spine, all slack and drooping in a dark box, with his legs doubled up round his neck, and not one of his social qualities remaining."[3] The description is disturbingly rendered in vaguely human terms, even as Punch's woodenness is being affirmed. And we listen as Dicken's mountebank, pausing to repair his company of puppets, proclaims "it wouldn't do to let 'em [the audience] see the present company undergoing repair. . . . Because it would destroy all the delusion, and take away all the interest."[4] Of course what these passages make clear is that in Dickens's fiction—and as we shall discover similarly in Aiken's—much of the "interest" is not mimetic, but is in the "delusion" itself and its relation to more commonplace realities.[5] We are invited to see the illusion, the expected realities framing it inside the work, and often the fictive machinery that brings the two together into yet another, larger fiction that is to be located in terms of the reader's "normal" world outside the work. As José Ortega y Gasset, writing of Cervantes, explained the working of fictional worlds:

The frame of the puppet show which Master Pedro goes around presenting is the dividing line between two continents of the mind. Within, the puppet show encloses a fantastic world, articulated by the genius of the impossible. It is the world of adventure, of imagination, of myth. Without there is a room in which several unsophisticated men are gathered, men like those we see every day, concerned with the daily struggle to live. . . . Nothing prevents us from entering this room: we could breathe in its atmosphere and touch those present on the shoulder, since they are made of the same stuff and condition as ourselves. However, this room is, in its turn, included in a book, that is to say, in another puppet show larger than the first. . . . [F]rom the puppet show to the room, from the room to the puppet show. One would say that the important thing is precisely the osmosis and endosmosis between the two.[6]

As befits a poem in which poetic play with fictive possibilities is of the utmost importance, Aiken's "Punch" was not composed systematically. It did not move directly toward some narrative goal either at its inception or later, when it was being pulled together for publication. As Aiken explained to Amy Lowell on 3 August 1921:

I am delighted that you think the characters are sustained . . . and that you like the epilogue and the general "arrangements." The latter business . . . was the problem of problems: the poem grew slowly and irregularly, and not in its present order. When the parts were complete I found, after much trial and error, the present, and I think on the whole the right, arrangement. The only sections of which the positions were "fixed" were the Two Old Men and the Epilogue. The real question was as to whether the bombast (the illusion, rather) should precede the analysis, or vice versa. In this respect my final order was my first—the first things written were What Punch Told Them and He Conceives His Puppet to be Struggling with a Net . . . and after that the poem was put aside for the writing of Senlin and then again taken up and slowly "filled out." (SL, 58-59)

In the final order full "analysis" came late, but when it came it told us what the title and several parts of the narrative had already implied—and what we had surely by then suspected: that the poem is about the limits and possibilities of creating and perceiving in circumstances the given of which is that every puppet has his master and every master his puppet strings.

Let us examine the last and the first parts of the poem. As Aiken's puppeteer—the maker and manipulator within the poem— steps from behind his stage to close up shop, he pauses to reflect on a situation that applies clearly to Aiken, the showman behind the whole show, as well as to himself and the show within the poem. For pages the reader has been made to wonder—albeit within the context of seeing the poem as a fiction—about the "reality" of a number of characters, varying from Punch's bar-room buddies to such literary figures as Faustus and Solomon and Sheba. Were the latter simply figments of Punch's dreamscape, fragments appearing out of the haze of his drunken boasts to impress other more tangible characters of the show? Are they fan-tasies within a fantasy? Or are they meant to be real characters in their own right? There is too the question of Punch's reality, and of course the question of the reality of the world the mysterious Punch enters as the poems begins.

TWO OLD MEN WHO REMEMBERED PUNCH

Do I remember Punch?—Listen—I'll tell you.
I am an old man now, but I remember,
I saw him in the flesh. . . .

. . . .

His great red nose was bent down like an ogre's,
His mouth was wide, he was half-bald, half-grey,
His legs were bandy. . . .

(CP, 300)

Who saw Punch come to town? Who was his father?
Where did he come from? ... Ah! You see; he's human,
(Or so you'd say,) yet no one ever knew
Just who he was, or what his business was.

(CP, 302)

Who is the "I" that sees Punch? To whom does he talk, seeming to imply that the reader-listener shares an experience of his world? On what ground does the reader stand? Does the reader participate in a mimetically intended fiction, a stage melodrama that for a moment here or there tricks him into disappearing into and then out of illusions of the real as he knows it? Or if Punch is but a puppet, as we knew before the poem began and as the tradi-tional descriptions of his physique and many of his actions remind us throughout the poem, then how do the old man and his cronies whom we meet later in the poem (if, of course, they *are* men) manage not to see it—or to convince us that it isn't so? Our answers point simply to the nature of fictions: in a show within a show, establishing reality is less important than understanding that there are questions to be asked and that regardless of the answers, what we come to appreciate is creative vitality that has energy of language, complexity of action—in short its own life.

In the epilogue to "Punch," the reader is no longer a listener sharing the narrator's direct address with other unnamed listeners, participating somehow in their world. Instead he seems to eavesdrop, at last seeing things from a distance in their "proper" perspective, or stepping within the puppet master's mind to perceive not his "art" but his motives for creating.

In the blue twilight the puller of strings, half-tenderly
Tumbling his puppets . . .
. . . .
. . . into their box, the cords relaxed,
The small world darkened, whereupon they danced
   and squeaked,—
Leaving them there in the dusk pell-mell together;
And turning away, at last, to look from a window
At a darker and greater world, ring beyond ring
Of houses and trees and stars . . .

. . . .

He saw himself,—though a god,—the puppet of gods;
Revolving in antics the dream of a greater dreamer;
. . . .
Was he no better than Judy, or Polly,—or Punch,
Capering about his cage of twittering dreams? . . .
                (CP, 360-61)

The voice of the puppeteer has become the voice of the poet; we are discovering the inner mechanism not only of the sideshow carny man but also of the artist who made him, and was made by another.

I too am a puppet. And as you are a symbol for me
(As Punch is, and Sheba—bright symbols of intricate meanings,
Atoms of soul—who move, and are moved by, me—)
So I am a symbol, a puppet drawn out upon strings,
Helpless, well-coloured, with a fixed and unchanging expression
. . . of some one who leans
Above me, as I above you ... And even this Some one,—
Who knows what compulsion he suffers, what hands out
    of darkness
Play sharp chords upon him! ... Who knows if those
    hands are not ours! ...

                                        (CP, 361-62)

   Puppets all, we manage by the poem's end to recognize and
acknowledge aesthetic and experiential possibilities—an
awareness made especially important by the strong sense that
finally emerges of the limits that frame possibilities. For the poet
there are the pleasures of literary play; for the reader, finally the
pleasure of joining in the game, providing the necessary audience
participation. A sophisticated artist acting as a theatrical showman, Aiken works his readers like a shell game huckster, continually confusing, directing, and misdirecting his audience with
flamboyant language, incongruous comparisons and satiric
antics, extravagant variations on comfortable literary contexts
we think we know. He manipulates the expectations created by
previous reading, without trying to hide the fact that he is twisting and turning these established conventions after he has made
us expect them. We perceive formulae and their insufficiency
almost at the same time; we are compelled to reflect on the relationship of teller to tale, character to character and to creator.
Perhaps in the end there are only shells—no pea, no object of
"truth" to which all the actions point. But observing the manipulator has been a delight, and we are left with a meaningful and
affirming creation: the performance itself.
   Poe-like, the narrator draws his readers together to tell them a
tale of fright and terror. Shadowy loomings and gothic grotes-
queries abound as the speaker, who seems in the phrase of Con-

rad's Marlow to declare himself "one of us," commands
immediate attention with direct address.

> So that's your story, is it?—Well, here's mine!
> Draw close your coats about you, cross yourselves—
> And shut the door! There's a queer wind tonight
> Howling as if some ghost were riding on it—
> Whose ghost, God knows! And what I've got to tell you
> Might crack the earth, and set the devil talking.
>
> (CP, 301)

With teeth chattering in the best gestural tradition, we huddle
against the imagined storm and revel in the terror of a good scare.
But fright is mixed with humor, presumably unintended by the
speaker. For Aiken, his tongue at times planted firmly but subtly
in his cheek, seems to enjoy having his narrator tell us more than
he thinks he does. Controlling the whole show, Aiken selects narrative details that seem less intended to make us cower than to
make us smile at the incongruities that we can perceive but the
narrator cannot. At key moments of tension, the poet reminds us
that the tale of terror is, after all, built on a splintery foundation
of puppets, and therefore may not neatly correspond to expectations raised by the gothic mode. Consider our first glimpses of
Punch:

> who saw Punch come to town? ...
> . . . .
> Old Crabbe it was—dead now these fifteen years—
> And he it was who told me. . . .
> . . . .
> He climbed the wall that joins the churchyard wall
> And skirts the road, and sat there, legs a-dangling,
> To peel a stick. Now then, you know that wall—
> . . . .
> . . . Well, Crabbe was whittling there,
> . . . .
> . . . And then, of a sudden,

Without a squeak or sound, another shadow
Slanted across the road and fell on the wall
Beyond his own,—and staid there ... Arms in the air,
Young Crabbe went stiff with fright; he turned his head
And saw in the road, alone before him,—Punch!
Punch, with a bag and stick across one shoulder—
And a red grin on his face! ...

                              Well—that was queer:
And young Crabbe felt his entrails coiling coldly.
                                        (CP, 302-3)

On one hand, our familiar world ("you know that wall") suddenly rendered alien is unsettling. Well might we begin to feel a
chill of fear were we not enjoying so much the unspecific
reminders—from legs dangling over walls, to whittling wood—
of the puppetry at the base of these horrors. Without a direct allu-
sion to Punch's wooden origins, Aiken has changed the weather
from gothic gloom to ironic glow, as the reader realizes that the
illusion-reality puzzle at the core of the thriller is more complex
than he had surmised.

The twists and turns of the poet's play continue as young-old
Crabbe notices, at an instant, "A thing that made his hair stand
up and creep" (CP, 303):

The road, of course, was dusty at that season,—
And Punch's boots showed not a speck of dust ...
This was enough! He slid back over the wall
And took the short-cut home.
                                        (CP, 304)

While Crabbe's hair rises, our own, after a tingle or two, is likely
to lie down at last. Aiken is managing to have it all ways on his
poetic stage; spinning a good, sometimes scarifying yarn, he
makes us comprehend the power of good storytelling. He makes
us think, too, while pondering Punch's dark origins, of larger

philosophical issues (the mysteries of motives for action, of moral behavior).

Consider then ... A mystery comes among us
Ugly and vile beyond all human knowledge,
. . . .
. . . Corruption rules us.

(CP, 304)

And by undercutting both his tale and his message with hints of the fictive machinery, strings and all, behind the poem (indeed we might well wonder why any well-cared-for, self-respecting, well-boxed puppet *should* have a dusty boot), the poet makes us aware of his own pleasure as shaper and shape-shifter at play with the possibilities of his craft.

The poem gets more complicated as Aiken, in the best ghost tale tradition, elaborates on Punch's earthly and supraearthly villainies: braggart, stalker of feminine virtue, gallows cheat, companion of many of tradition's greatest boundary-breakers (Faustus, Heliogabalus, Sheba, Judas, even Satan), Christ-denier, and devil-cheater. And complexity multiplies further as Aiken probes, from differing points of view, the implications of the various psychoses expressed by Punch in his need to feel self-important (physically as sexual conqueror of Judy, Polly, even Sheba, and intellectually as champion in cunning over Faustus, the hangman Jack Ketch, Solomon, the Devil himself). Aiken renders it all in "What Punch Told Them," "What Polly Once Confessed," and in the very different view of Mountebank, who while he "Carves His Puppet of Wood / . . . Conceives His Puppet To Be Struggling With A Net" (CP, 308, 330, 338). Still the poem, so self-consciously a manipulation of ideas of unearthly horror with ridiculous buffoonery and playful embellishment, leaves us, in the wake of its galloping rhythms and images, with a sense of having been a witness to a masterfully playful flexing of poetic muscle. Here is an elaboration of poetic possibility that finally makes us suspect that the poet's voice is clearest in Punch's exclamation: "Oh, Lord, oh, Lord, what things I've done! / What tricks have played, what devil's fun" (CP, 316).

4 Legends, Dreams, and Graphic Grotesqueries
"John Deth: A Metaphysical Legend"

We have been discovering in "Punch" the beginnings of an expression of the genre that John Ruskin defined in "The Grotesque Renaissance" as

in almost all cases, composed of two elements, one ludicrous, the other fearful; that, as one or the other of these elements prevails, the grotesque falls into two branches, sportive grotesque and terrible grotesque; but that we cannot legitimately consider it under these two aspects, because there are hardly any examples which do not in some degree combine both elements; there are few grotesques so utterly playful as to be overcast with no shade of fearfulness, and few so fearful as absolutely to exclude all ideas of jest.[1]

This is a way of seeing that George Santayana explained in 1896 in *The Sense of Beauty* as "an interesting effect produced by such a transformation of an ideal type as exaggerates one of its elements or combines it with other types."[2] In *Past Masters* Thomas Mann identified the genre as "broadly and essentially, the striking feature of modern art," which had, he felt,

ceased to recognize the categories of tragic and comic, or the dramatic classifications, tragedy and comedy. It sees life as tragi-comedy, with the result that the grotesque is its most genuine style—to the extent, indeed, that today that is the only guise in which the sublime may appear. For, if I may say so, the grotesque is the genuine anti-bourgeois style; and however bourgeois Anglo-Saxondom may otherwise be or appear, it is a fact that in art the comic-grotesque has always been its strong point.[3]

Of course, this art of clashing contraries, reacting somewhat

against middle-class forms and habits—and in the reaction help-
ing to sketch in and define middle-class boundaries as well—is
not simply the aesthetic of "the modern." It constitutes an important part of the art of Hieronymus Bosch, Pieter Breughel, Hans
Holbein, Albrecht Dürer, Charles Dickens, and Robert Browning, as well as of Joseph Conrad, Franz Kafka, James Joyce, Sher-
wood Anderson, and Samuel Beckett. But it represents a pre-
dominant perception in our century, and it was to serve Aiken
perfectly throughout the 1920s as he sought, with ever-increasing
intensity, to find ways of expressing and explaining the possibilities and limits of artistic form.

The Albert Camus remarked that "absurdity" was the essential feature in a world in which there seem to be no explanations, in
which we all feel like aliens "deprived of the memory of a lost
home or the hope of a promised land."[4] But Aiken, though feeling
himself *Among the Lost People,* as he was to call his third volume
of short stories (1934), refused to consider the home or the promise lost. In fact, his writing was from the first—and remained to
the end—a search for an affirmation of both the stability of an
idea of home and the promise of a place to come. Still, he
expressed uncompromisingly the chaos that marks the vision of
the modern.

The grotesque, as an art with a comfortably long tradition,
permitted Aiken a version of an aesthetic order that by definition
both acknowledged and partially shaped disorder. For grotesque
art is nothing so much as an attempt to invoke, and yet render less
dangerous and threatening, the abnormal—the primordial
images representing the anxieties, deviations, and nightmares of
a whole culture, or the bogies from the demonic regions of the
solitary mind. In all cases the grotesque is a way of seeing the
world that acknowledges the terrifying, even while disarming it
through humor that to an extent trivializes it in the light of
altered perspective. As Wolfgang Kayser has written, in the most
effective grotesque the "darkness has been sighted, the ominous
powers discovered, the incomprehensible forces challenged."[5]
The grotesque never abandons the "normal" completely; instead
it establishes and distorts a notion of original form, throwing the

reader so off his balance that he is torn between a desire to hide from the terrors he sees so clearly and to laugh at their incongruity. According to Lee Byron Jennings:

A type of situation can be conceived of that displays a deep-seated distortion with aspects of the fearsome and ludicrous, where absurdity runs rampant. . . . The familiar structure of existence is undermined and chaos seems imminent. This aspect is intensified when concrete manifestations of decay appear and a feeling of hopelessness and corruption is developed. The ludicrous aspect, in turn, arises from the farcical quality inherent in such scenes of absurdity and approaching chaos. A feeling of detachment arises as we become absorbed in wonderment at the unfolding of unheard-of-events. Thus, the disarming function is again in evidence; the threat of chaos brings with it a terrifying vertigo and loss of footing, but the footing is regained as we attain the . . . vantage point of the observer.[6]

Knowing that we are confronting an established genre, which is defined by the depiction of dissolution and the accompanying confusions of horror and humor, still does not enable the reader to gain a point of intellectual distance, just as knowing the category of tragedy does not permit one to feel the catharsis any less. In fact, the sense of recognizing a type of literature even while succumbing to its seeming disorders simply accentuates the complicated multiplicity of responses that accompany the disorientations.

When we speak of grotesque variations from a norm, we may be referring to objects, individuals, situations, perhaps even grotesque worlds. Aiken's poem "John Deth: A Metaphysical Legend" presents its distortions on all these levels. The "facts" explaining the creation of the poem turn on a chance comic discovery that Aiken made while living in Winchelsea, England, in 1922. While reading a borrowed book of local history he found that among the early grantees of land under the auspices of royal charter in the late thirteenth century were John Deth, Juliana Goatibed, and Millicent Piggistaile.[7] The poem's curiously unliterary inspiration is somehow right, considering the final mixture of emotional and intellectual modes and responses, yet it is wildly inappropriate for the poem's weighty philosophical intention. As Aiken described in a letter to Robert Linscott in May 1924:

In the present work, I recognize many of the characteristics which have invited objections to the other poems. First and foremost, the fact that it is in essence a parable, and that the meaning is so deeply hidden and embedded in the poem, and so nihilistic when discovered, that by some it will be disliked for its themelessness and by some for its morbidity. Superficially, the parable can be said to state that a great part of the effort of life is an effort to die; that consciousness is a disease of Matter, an abnormality, and that a part of consciousness knows this, and, like the Sibyl, wishes to die, to return into unconsciousness. A very simple and very comforting idea. In the poem, John Deth and Millicent Piggistaile represent the positive and negative poles of life (the terms should be reversed); and "love," or Venus, is the will or force that moves them. The other figure, Juliana Goatibed, in a sense contains them, is the sum of them, is their consciousness: it is through her that Deth and Millicent know their slavery and misery, and desire, by crucifixion of Venus, to obtain peace. In the allegorizing of this idea, there had to be and are certain imaginative loosenesses; the scheme need not be pressed too hard. What, in short, I have tried to do is to make on the one hand a poem which can be taken simply as a fantastic myth and, on the other, one which will yield, on scrutiny, a profound meaning. (SL, 92-93)

The title of the poem's early version, "The Dance of Deth,"[8] gives us a fine hint of ways to comprehend the coherence of myth and meaning, extravagant fantasy and probing Freudianism.[9] For "John Deth" is a poem in motion, and its motion of a dance, both patterned and undisciplined, is characteristic of much grotesque art. The tensions of regularity with sudden awkward movements within the frame of a pattern unbalance the reader, making him aware that both dancer and dance are irregular. The work presents a spectacle for our contemplation, an unnerving parade of both recognizable types and shocking shapes and figures, which like the traditional skeleton dances of art and literature breaks down boundaries of the living and the dead even as they are defined.

That Aiken's poem was highly self-conscious, meticulously

worked over, is clear from a letter to Robert Linscott in October
1924:

> I burst with the news that I have now revised the Dance of Deth and will
> immediately send it to you in its new form. . . . Parts one and two are
> greatly changed, and I think for the better, and I am grateful to you for
> your firm and heartless advice. Parts three four and five remain as they
> were. I tried to change Part three (birds) and even recast several of the
> birdsongs; but everywhere I met (as the war communiqués used to say)
> with determined resistance; I found the octosyllabic structure so stub-
> bornly compact in all the second half of the poem that every change was
> for the worse, and I eventually gave it up. The opening, too, gave me no
> end of trouble. The present one is the sixth, and I am not yet sure of it. It
> seemed to me that something slow and sombre, a little heavy, was
> wanted; heroic couplets didn't quite do it, nor irregular couplets; so I
> have now begun with blank verse, shifting after five lines into rhyme.
> (WU, 5 October 1924)

Still, the early impressions we get of the propulsive rhythms and
rhymes suggest a storyteller at his ease:

John Deth and his doxies came to town.
By the weeping-cross they sank them down.
. . . .
Hurry! and at the Star-Tree tavern
Rouse the musicians; have the seven
Fiddles playing, and devil's drum,
To jig to ... Tell them that I come.

                              (CP, 397)

With a kind of vaudevillian vigor,[10] the narrator piles up details
and kaleidoscopic images of person and place, laying out before
us, as he does so, frame after episodic frame that remind us of
well-known jigs like Hans Holbein's *Danse Macabre,* Thomas
Rowlandson's *The English Dance of Death* series, and the crowd
scenes of William Hogarth's *The March to Finchley, Southwark
Fair,* and *Industry and Idleness.* It is in the brief, general comfort
that comes from the echoes of familiar artistic territory, together
with the immense, cluttered energy in the depiction of individual
details of figure and place, that Aiken is able to work his magic
with the grotesque.

Imbued with a *sense of* knowing where we are, and forgetting for a moment—distracted by the fascination of extravagant detail—to ask where we are going, we find ourselves suddenly doubly dislocated. The details we have been observing so closely are sufficiently distorted to prevent our feeling comfortable with them: inanimate things come to life and are thrown together with presumably sentient beings, which are suddenly disanimated; body parts are distorted through exaggeration or diminution; and the narrative seems unexpectedly to have taken us to a scene that, caught off guard as we are, startles and terrifies us. Though each episode finally does make clear the connectives in motives, actions, and descriptions, preparing us for scenes to come and linking us to scenes already past, these links are scarcely realized until we are past the scene at hand and are into another episode, which has its own reflexive interest. Thus, only after having finished the opening stanza do we realize that, in fact, we do not know quite where we are in space (what town do the travellers come to? where and what are the Star-Tree Tavern and the cross that weeps?) or what complexities the narrator may have been suggesting about the interrelationships of the characters (what will be the implications of Deth's addressing Juliana as "a mind put by"?). And even these questions register as a kind of mental double take, for by the time we note them we are already caught up in the barrage of details and events that follow—each one interesting us in its own right firstly, and only secondarily as part of the whole narrative, dancing with such energy that we can barely follow the steps even though we know they are there.

> "For John Deth comes
> To beat his feet to the beating drums."
> (CP, 401)

> the dance so deeply learned:
> The dance of bones that beat and burned.
> (CP, 407)

We observe with Deth:

The crablike moon thrust out a claw,
Wave at a sea-weed cloud, and swim
In a blue pool; then dive and dim.

                                    (CP, 398)

We marvel at the bizarre new beast created by this mixture of astronomy and zoology in which characteristics of one form of nature seem transferred to another. The peculiar animation of the moon, willfully thrusting and waving, then diving, is also, we realize, simply a description of a crescent moon reflected in a pool of water. Once it has been beasted, however, it will not be merely moon again. Having sprung to life in our mind's eye, the moon will remain part sentient animal even if we realize that the transformation is the result of metaphoric language—or even if we realize that the description represents a kind of psychological dislocation. We soon see that the image of the claw is one of John Deth's defining characteristics—making him more than a metaphysical concept, perversely humanizing and dehumanizing him at once, and rendering him a figure of life-in-death:

                              Elaine
. . . .
You'd live once more, to dance with me,—
To kiss my claw—

                                    (CP, 399)

Clawlike again became the hand
That stiffly held the flowering wand.

                                    (CP, 405)

Deth raised once more the clawlike hand
That bore the moon-white-flowered wand;
. . . .
With each sharp hiss a petal dropped
In withered grass.

                                    (CP, 408)

The transference of the characterizing feature—the claw—to the

moon calls our attention to the complex perceptual and psychological relationship between an observer and a thing observed, in
which one's perception is shaped as much by what he is as by what
is there: a clawlike Deth sees a clawlike moon. In a broader way, it
implies too that in the world of the poem images of death are pervasive, infecting every thing and every place. The near-simultane-
ous concurrence of perceptual, psychological, and philosophical
impressions leaves the reader discomfited. Uncertain of how to re-
act, he is scarcely ready to proceed, but the poetic pace is relentless.

Frightening and ludicrous characters beat their feet by us,
revealed in impossible events and descriptions. Deth limps and
scampers, loathes and loves:

St. Mary's laboring clock he saw
Measuring hard the double law
Of life and death . . .
Dust and breath . . .
. . . .
Darkly dreaming, he caused to fall
One pebble from the rotting wall.
He felt it strike, in his deep brain;
And shrank, as one who shrinks from pain.
                    (CP, 399-400)

To an extent, this part of the poem is Deth's nightmare, as perhaps
he is Aiken's and ours. We have come a long way from the stagey
melodrama of "Punch." The images of terror are more complex.
Our grimaces and confusions at this scene—walls rotting in the
middle of undefined space and objects penetrating figuratively or
literally into brains that may or may not be intended to have physical substance—are accentuated when we discover the impossible
figure of "Petronilla . . . / Under her cobweb tent of hair" (CP,
398) just waking in "A wilderness of rusted graves" (CP, 399). Yet
grimaces are jostled by nervous smiles as unsettling images mix
with good-humored, satiric typing. As if from the pages of an eigh-
teenth-century farce, we find a bishop passing "with a caper."

Behind him tripped the sad-eyed vicar
Who beamed on Millicent, the liquor

Seething his blood to frothy ichor.
"Come, Millicent, my spangled queen!
Come thump your shivering tambourine—
And dance me to the realm unseen!"

                              (CP, 401)

The linguistic energy is contagious, and we find ourselves
caught up by the thumping, seething rhythm, only to discover
that in enjoying and giving ourselves over to the motions we too
have become part of the grotesque transformation. Like some
cavorting serpentine creature, newly wakened and come to life,
the dancers—and to an extent the readers—prance past on their
frenzied way toward death. They are ludicrous when viewed as
cartoonlike individuals, a bizarre rhythmic monster when seen in
their common identity.

In wavering row the rout came dancing;
Now backwards drawn, and now advancing;
And Deth, with delicate wand, caressed
Each, as he came, on brow or breast:
. . . .
Juliana and aproned Barlyng;
The toothless Vicar; and his darling
Millicent, the spangled queen,
Beating aloft her tambourine;
. . . .
And last of all, with Doctor Lewd
Elaine; who, weeping as he wooed,—
Led out in his obscene embrace,—
Covered with shameful hands her face.
. . . .
After them all, gaunt-shadowed Deth.

. . . .
With angry claw he waved away
The Star-Tree sign, the Star-Tree Inn;
And laughed, to see his feet begin
Themselves the dance so deeply learned:
The dance of bones that beat and burned.

                              (CP, 406-7)

Located and dislocated by our impressions, realizing the strange ways the consciousness comes to an awareness of itself and the world as we struggle to make simple sense out of a barrage of feelings, we find ourselves before too long in the most disturbingly grotesque scene of all. As a kind of afterthought we realize that the narrator's energized descriptions of the demonic dance have been readying us for this moment, and yet we cannot be prepared for the specificity of the physical distortions or for the stark explicitness of the psychological insights into the ways death and life are mixed. We confront a moment of bizarre sexual intensity, which has certainly been felt as an undercurrent of the poem all along and which reads like an exploration of the fearsome implications of the account of nature's reciprocity found earlier in "Senlin."

At the poem's dark center, Deth and Millicent come together. The violence of the images of sexual encounter—the thrusting, cracking, knotting, scraping, and tearing—freezes us in our uneasy laughter at the irregularity of the advance of death's heaving conga line. Here is Deth's own dance of desire, and its destructive copulative force, which perversely mingles sterility and desire, destruction and creation, tells us indeed that finding "the core of anguish, underground" (CP, 412) is inevitably linked to the growth of the "world-bearing tree" (CP, 413) of adult knowledge and life.

1
"This night," said Deth, "I lie with you:
Our deathless sorrow we renew.
I'll see once more, through your deep face,
The horror huge of ruined space—
Where all that grew no longer grows;

. . . .
There will I lie! there slowly thrust
Dead roots, to crack that sterile dust."

. . . .

2
. . . Millicent and Deth,

In the black yew-tree shadow, strove
To warm in bone and rock their love.
There Millicent lay back, and pressed
Deth's scythe-sharp chin against her breast
As though to cut, with that bright bone,
Into her heart of hollow stone.
. . . .
. . . Here thrust and knot your roots.

. . . .

3

. . . .
And there, upthrust in dripping gloom,
A black, dishonored, cracking tomb.
And on the tomb there grew a tree
Which moved its white roots rapidly
. . . .
. . . a taproot whistling thrust
Into the sighing vault of dust
And swelled and reddened and rived apart
The aching stones and pierced the heart;
. . . .
. . . Then cried aloud
The injured tomb: "Your roots have found
The core of anguish, underground!
My inward walls they search and scrape
And I am blest! ... My lord, what shape
Take you above? And do you grow?"
The dark tree answered: "Grief I know,
And feed on. . . .
. . . .
Swiftly I grow! My branches turn
Like burning boughs that as they burn
Twist upward through the twisting fire
And feed upon it as on desire."

(CP, 410-12)

The womb-tomb message, so heavily marked by Freudianism
for the 1920s, is of course as old as literature itself. Yet in extending the procedure of continually mixing modes and impressions,

Aiken has made the message work by providing both the distance needed for comprehending the point intellectually and the closeness needed to grasp it viscerally. The combination of the extremely particular detailing of unheard-of things and the myth-making expansiveness in the descriptions leaves the reader no precise vantage. There is enough focus to allow him to grasp the event analytically as a cultural phenomenon, and enough direct contact to feel it as a very real, immediate experience, a kind of private sexual nightmare. But caught again in the shifting perceptual and emotional currents of the poem, at once close and distant, the reader is still threatened by the vertigo that will spin him loose from all stability.

Therefore, in the poem's last sections Aiken, having managed to exhaust his reader with explorations of poetic and perceptual possibilities, urges his reader away from grotesquery and discovery toward fable and recovery of equilibrium. He continues to present dislocating transformations but mixes these increasingly with a more straightforward didactic parable. Deth, looking to extend his destructive force, seeks among far-flying birds an answer to the questions: "Where's beauty fled? Where's brightness lying?" (CP, 422).

> Then spoke the owl: "Tuwhoo! ...
> Last night by China Wall I flew.
> I saw Confucius lapt in red
> Among the brown Cataian dead.
> 'Beauty is in the mind,' he said."
> (CP, 423)

> Then sang the thrush: . . .
> . . . .
> "She, lord, is beauty, who can make
> So grievously dead earth to wake!"
> (CP, 424, 425)

The thrust of Aiken's fable is simple, and rendered clearly. He explained it further in a letter to Houston Peterson on 5 October 1928:

Piggistaile is a plus sign, Deth is a minus sign: Goatibed is their coeffi-
cient. They are doomed to an infinite and wearisome repetition of their
ritual. They all hate it. If they can seize on and annihilate the *principle* of
the affair,—Venus,—they can end it. They crucify Venus (reference
obvious enough to Jesus and the Adonis myth etc.) in the hope of getting
rid of the whole affair. But, as suggested at the end of the poem, this *is* an
illusion. The thing will go on. . . . It will perform itself over and over
again, this world being what it is. There will always be Piggistailes and
Deths, with their concomitant Goatibed. The plus will always attack the
minus, marry it and produce consciousness, Goatibed, who will want to
be *un*conscious ... Thus wrapped up in a fairy story . . . the poem.[11]

Having chosen his details, as he said, with an "affective eye, with
a view to as much reference to the human scene as possible: historical as well as psychological,"[12] Aiken manages a poetic *tour
de force*. Careful, finally, to make sure that we *know* what we
have felt, he presents a parabolic gloss in the poem's final sections: "The Falling of the Birds," "Venus Anadyomene," and
"Juliana Goatibed."

>   Venus, goddess of Love,
> · · · · · · · · · · · · · · · ·
> She, lord, is beauty!
> ("The Falling of the Birds," CP, 433)

> "Think not, my people, the god is dead,
> ·
> Twisting in death, and burning, I
> Live in the hearts that crucify ..."
>   ("Venus Anadyomene," CP, 440)

>   And there she saw
> · · · · · · · · · · · · · · · · · ·
> Deth sleeping, but about to wake;
> Millicent, weeping for his sake;
> Herself beside them, wide-eyed, weaving
> Vision of peace beyond believing ...
> ·
> Her mind grew dark. The world was dead.
> She dreamed.
>   ("Juliana Goatibed," CP, 443)

But Aiken offers his explication only after the reader has been made to experience directly the complicated physical and psychological realities that make the message meaningful. Concretely and suggestively, then, in "John Deth" Aiken has extended his experiments with poetic form to enable him to recreate and articulate predicaments, both social and private, in the stages of man's evolving consciousness.

5 Vaudevillians and Doctors, Minds and Bodies

"Changing Mind" and "The Coming Forth by Day of Osiris Jones"

If the focus of the grotesque in "John Deth" is broad, essentially relating to a whole culture, the grotesque in "Changing Mind," written at about the same time and later added to *The Divine Pilgrim,* is more particularized.[1] Instead of hinting at private meanings within the context of a poem whose subject is not individualized, "Changing Mind" generalizes outward from close attention to a specific psychic being. And "The Coming Forth by Day of Osiris Jones" (1931), written as a new decade got under way, focuses on minute details of a world of objects, complementing nicely the mind's-eye view of "Changing Mind." Each poem takes for its starting point one kind of seeing, interior or exterior. Together the poems embody fifteen years of Aiken's explorations into the complex relationships between subjective and objective perceptions.

In a 1949 preface to the republication of "Changing Mind," Aiken wrote that the poem provides *The Divine Pilgrim* series with what

might be called the specific "I," and at a specific moment in its experience, in a specific predicament: the predicament, both private and social, of the writer or artist. Senlin is the purely racial examplar—the basic stock reacting to basic situations. He is the inheritor of racial memories, and through these of even deeper instinctual responses, but beyond this he is not particularized. . . . The wholly anonymous hero of "Changing Mind," on the other hand . . . is not only particularized, he is also shown to be the willing participant, and perhaps to some extent even the instigator, in the process of seeing himself resolved into his constituent particles. . . . Not only does he inherit the ordinary basic

48

unconscious memory of Senlin—he also inherits the complete private situation of a highly complex and self-conscious contemporary individual whose neuroses have made it necessary or desirable that he should be an artist. He must make his experience articulate for the benefit of others, he must be, in the evolving consciousness of man, the servant-example. (CP, 1024-25)

Remembering Santayana's observation that the poet "dips into the chaos that underlies the rational shell of the world"[2] to fetch his poetic wares, we discover, in the portrait of the "I" of the poem, the shapes of the irrational dream and the ways these shapes are inevitably mixed up perceptually with the outlines of the rational world. As Aiken explained it to his close friend, psychiatrist George B. Wilbur on 2 January 1931:

Changing Mind might interest you . . . built on a series of dreams, with simply the notion of portraying the mind in a moment of affective transition—an adjustment, symbolically, to a highly painful group of memories and recognitions. (SL, 167)

The poem invites us, almost immediately, below consciousness into the fluid world of the unconscious, where bizarre figures from within the psyche mingle with oddly refracted images from the world of consciousness above. The fusions and jarring juxtapositions create a world where abnormality and normality collide, sharing a common terrain uncomfortably, each making us rethink the nature of the other as we perceive them together in the new, strange environment. In an ambiguously defined room, "filled with the sound of voices, . . . weaving like vines. / . . . / Moving like golden water" (SP, 67), we are asked with the personae to "Come down under the talk" (SP, 68). Aiken's care in giving the mental world a physical concreteness, as if the places behind the eye had their own literal boundaries and configurations—"Stoop your shoulders / And enter the darkness" (SP, 68)—makes it impossible for us to avoid issues of perceptual reality by rendering a simple symbolic translation of the poem. Given a sense of physical location but without enough information to feel comfortable in our surroundings, we are made to accept the invitation. While the voices from "out there" fade in and out of range, we dive into the simultaneously frightening and protecting darkness of a womblike, interior world. Here we discover that the world of light partakes of the darkness within, even as the dark world of impulse seems partially to shape the brighter world of reason.

The poet-personae, plunging "under the four-voiced dialogue" (SP, 68) of mother, father, lover, and psychoanalyst, seeks to escape, in a moment of complete narcissistic self-absorption, the psychic claims of those who want to objectify him. He longs to avoid those who would "separate him out / Into a handfull of blank syllables" dispersing him as a man of words: "Dissected out on the glass-topped table, / The tweezers picking up syllables and putting them down, / Particles so small they have no colour" (SP, 69).

> "Come under!" he said;
> And as he spoke I saw him! . . .
> . . . .
> His white arms, curving like a swimmer's, shaped
> The dark sphere out of brightness. There he curled,
> In that cold chrysalis, secret under the talk,
> Carved in the light.
>
> "You! Narcissus!" I said!
> And softly, under the four-voiced dialogue,
> In the bright ether, in the golden river
> Of cabbalistic sound, I plunged, I found
> The silver rind of peace, the hollow round
> Carved out of nothing; curled there like a god.
>   (SP, 68)

Distinct definitions of the realms of dark or light are collapsing already. The deliberate ambiguity of logic and language is so strong that we cannot even be certain if the place of peace is, in fact, under "the moving water" woven by "spider-mouths" (SP, 68). The plunge, after all, is "under" the dialogue, but "*in* the golden river" (my italics); and although this "river / Of cabbalistic sound" seems here to be the one created by the whisperings with Narcissus, a golden place wherein lies the source of a "silver rind of peace" that seems to represent complete escape from external voices, we remember that it was the exterior "torrent of talk" itself that was described only a few lines earlier as "Moving like golden water" (SP, 67). The early apparent emotional connotations of "golden" as dazzling but cold and dangerous, associated with the four-voiced stream, are suddenly indecipherable. Thoroughly disoriented spatially, analytically, emotionally, we are discovering that the outer voices and the inner voices are part of the same torrent.

The deliberate imagistic inconsistencies are further complicated by the account of one of the four speakers—the woman "whose long hair of burnt gold / Fell on the talk and was woven into it" (SP, 68)—as one whose "*glare* . . . [of] love" (my italics) has the power to "reassemble" (SP, 69) the dispersed narrator. Suddenly we cannot even be sure of the positive or negative implications of love or even of psychic disintegration, which had seemed so negative ("the tweezers picking up syllables and putting them down" [SP, 69]), but which for this moment seems no worse than being reassembled by the golden-haired woman's "sovereign eye" (SP, 69).

As Jonathan Culler has remarked, "To understand the language of a text is to recognize the world to which it refers."[3] Though such comprehension also may involve illogical impingements on the consciousness or may involve immediate responses to sound, image, and rhythm, the point is well taken; a part of all response to literature is to seek to "naturalize" a text, locating it in relation to some system of more conventional meanings (cultural, linguistic, generic) from which the creating act in part removed it by giving it its own formal energy and shape.[4] We find ourselves unsettlingly alienated in the worlds of "Changing Mind" precisely because, although we can recognize denotative and connotative references to physical and psychological systems we know, we are unable, finally, to make sense of the poem by relating it to a set of associations of words, objects, and meanings. Usual analytic and emotional associations with words like gold, silver, love, dispersal, dissection, dark, bright, light, or torrent are inadequate, or confused or inapplicable, and no system of signs and symbols within the poem is consistent enough to provide a needed temporary counternormal or fictive system of reference. Within the poem, any systems, associations, positives, or negatives are always changing, always unbalancing us as we move ourselves from assemblage to dispersal of meaning and emotional response, looking for our coherent resting place— our "silver rind of peace."

We find ourselves in our watery world at one moment dodging either derisive laughter or an incomprehensibly piercing whistling from the mysterious "small man" (SP, 69) (we discover him later as the father figure), and at another moment engrossed in a nightmarish sexual fantasy that mixes obvious Freudian and Biblical overtones into a kind of bent version of a Browning monologue. The recognizable physical and literary reference points only serve to make us more aware of the impossibility of the closely detailed scenes before us, which, though immediate and concrete, still refuse categorization. Neither simply metaphor nor symbol nor mimetic reality, the scenes render an intensely suffocating glimpse of an emotional complex realized when the poet's father figure names him "Inheritor" (SP, 71) of sexual knowledge and guilt, of suffering and of death.

> The small man whistled:
> After the four dull boulders of their laugh
> Had sunk beside me. . . .
> . . . The long whistle
> Ran like a nerve. . . .
> . . . .
> . . . This all four pressed at once
> And the long screaming nerve wound through the water,
> While they above it leaned. Ah, did they see
> How the blue nerve was grounded twice in me?
>
> (SP, 69)

> The small man brooded
> Darkly above me, darkly glowing,

Mephistopheles, holding in his wide hand
All these shapes. "It is the kite country,"
. . . .

"Childe Roland, leaving behind him the dark tower,
Came in the evening to the land of kites.
. . . .
He saw the diamond kites all rise at once . . .
. . . And on each kite was bound
A weeping woman, the arms outstretched, the feet
Nailed at the foot!"

              (Alas, how hard it is,
I helpless, bound thus, in my cave, asleep,
Bound in the stinging nerves of sound, these voices!)

. . . .
. . . "He climbs
Slowly in twilight to the weeping-cross ...
Alas, good woman, you no sooner lust
Together concupiscent, your four arms
Enwreathed, your faces fused in one, your eyes
Sightless with foresight of the two-backed beast,
Than with derisive cries and cruel eyes
The kiteflyers come! Your outstretched hands they nail
Against the Crosspiece! Then down the hill they run
Drawing the kitecord with them, so that, weeping,
He hears you, weeping, blown aloft in air!"

Thus the small man, amid derisive laughter!
                      (SP, 73-74)

    Often it is precisely the detail and language that we recognize
most clearly as having immediate reference in our commonplace
world that, when transformed by context, unsettles us most. For
example, we know that Aiken loved the energetic colloquialisms
of the comic stage, the comic strip, and the movies:

That [1910] was a wonderful period in the popular arts. I mean all kinds
of things, slang, the movies, the funnies. They were all at their best:

Krazy Kat, Mutt and Jeff, Rube Goldberg. There was an extraordinary
explosion of creative adventure during those years. Jazz and the movies
were coming along, vaudeville was at its peak. (Shenandoah, 25)

I was an addict of vaudeville, and Boston was marvelous for it. . . . It
was a wonderful mixture of vulgarity and invention, of high spirits and
dirty cracks. (PR, 116-17)

But when street-theater language finds its way into "Changing
Mind"—enabling Aiken to experiment at mixing linguistic
inventiveness with more formal poetic diction—we realize that
the poet is undermining its typical function even as he reminds us
of it, first "placing" us and finally, more violently, "displacing" us.
Thus a usual function of such linguistic high-jinks—as a kind of
escape from routine—is reversed, and the slang serves in this
strange poem first to remind us of "normalcy." After all, even
when the Lord of Misrule reigns, as on the vaudeville stage,
attending a performance is part of sanctioned social behavior. We
recognize the language and action formulas and for a moment
feel comfortable with them. But in the end, Aiken's use of vaudevillian routines makes us realize that the theatrical antics in their
transplanted context are terribly bizarre—comic, terrifying, and
incomprehensible. Our sense of alienation is greater than if we
had not felt somehow that this familiar—suddenly made
unfamiliar—routine had been designed for our amusement.

With what seems to be insufficient preparation, we find ourselves wrenched from the inscrutable world of psychic interiors
to the center stage of a vaudeville house, described in a somewhat
lurid magazine prose. We seem to have moved perceptually from
subjective to objective. The abrupt scene shift makes what follows register as the least logical moment in a poem full of abnormal happenings. (How did we get *here?* What has this to do with
where we have just been?) And yet the show and the setting for it
are fascinating enough in their own right to constitute a separate
territory that offers, too, a kind of touchstone for normalcy,
which the poem has not offered thus far. Within the context of
the poem we seem more displaced than ever. Outside that context, however, we find for the first time a kind of familiar loca-

tion—although paradoxically the theatrical place we recognize is itself, in "normal" contexts, one that is full of habitual abnormalities: painted faces, slapstick farce rituals, and so forth.

The seven-man orchestra tuned up bubbling and squeaking. Harry Frank, the conductor, stuffed a dirty handkerchief inside his collar, turning goggle eyes to see if his friend Anne was in the audience; and Tom, the drummer, with his prizefighter's mug, was chatting with a couple of skirts in the front row. Lights! Lights! O'Dwyer, his bloodshot eyes, looked round the cherubimed corner of the proscenium arch to see what they were waiting for. What were they waiting for? "Hearts and Flowers." Harry rapped his frayed bow on the lamplit tripod, turned his smug Jewish profile from Tom to O'Dwyer, sleekly smiling. He began briskly. The theatre was full. Three thousand faces. Faces in rows like flowers in beds. (SP, 74)

The scene, rendered with a sort of exaggerated melodramatic naturalism, captures our attention—as good theater or juicy reportage might—and seems to invite us thereby to forget for a moment the poem's psychic rumblings, as it fascinates us instead with the familiar (albeit peculiar) comic caricatures, broad gestures, and slambang colloquial verbal energy. How disconcerting, then, to discover the additional paradox that this theatricalism does not, however peculiar itself, belong primarily to the world outside the mind, that it does not, in fact, refer to a place beyond claustrophobic interior confusions but rather is Aiken's vehicle for providing a gloss to the confusions the reader has encountered thus far in the world behind the eye.

And all this, mind you, was myself! myself still asleep under the four-voiced dialogue! the fourfold river of talk! Here the three thousand faces leaned down upon me, stamens and pistils! and here I was the orchestra, a submarine orchestra, a telephone exchange of blue nerves, and a bare stage on which something was about to happen! (SP, 74)

Still, the scenes that unfold are so effective by themselves that even as we prepare to read them as a kind of key to the mysteries of the rest of the poem, we are submerged once more in the fascination of the language and cartoonlike actions and reactions.

We drift from contact with the poem as a whole into the world of theatrical entertainment, which itself turns nightmarish and disorienting both in its own right and as a measurement of the personae's interior being. What a perceptual mauling Aiken gives us, always in control of his poem and managing the almost miraculous feat of simultaneously locating and dislocating his reader both inside *and* outside of the poem.

Here I was Luvic, warbling, her white arms fat at the shoulders, like hams powdered. . . . Here I was Glozo, the card-eater, the ventriloquist, who took goldfish out of his gold-toothed mouth. . . . I was Bozo, the muscular trapeze artist, and all the while I was Harry cocking his left eye over his fiddle, and Tom rubbing sandpaper together (wisha wisha) while Mrs. Bishop put her perfumed hand in his pocket, and three thousand yellow faces perched in rows like birds, and a humming marble foyer with gilt mirrors. . . .

All this I was, and also the amphitheatre itself,
. . . .
All this I was, but also those four strangers
Leaning above me, leaning above the stream.
                              (SP, 74-75)

The grotesque parody of the artist's public appearances—yowling singer, many-voiced ventriloquist, heavy-drinking down-and-outer, trapeze risk-taker, orchestrator-conductor, audience and theater too—turns violent as the view of the nightmare darkens with the brutal, center-stage destruction of ego-Narcissus:

Bang! said the gong, and the red giant from his corner
Sprang to the ring, shaking the boards. The other
Rose terrified, submissive, his thin hands
Ungloved, his chin defenceless, and his heart
Visibly beating.

        "You! Narcissus!" I said!
And as I rose the giant's hard glove crashed

Black on the visible heart . . .

. . . .

. . . Then the applause, roaring like rain!

. . . .

My father, chill from the grave, leaned down and
   smiled.

. . . .

(. . . I ran to the dead man
And raised his head. Alas, what horror,
When I saw the chest-wall rotted, the heart
Hanging like a cluster of grapes,
Beating weakly, uncovered and sick.
Alas, too, what horror when he said:
Daily I fight here,
Daily I die for the world's delight
By the giant blow on my visible heart!)
                           (SP, 76-77)

"Let the poet . . . first of all *rediscover himself*" (CC, 102)
Aiken once wrote. "For surely the basis of *all* poetic activity, its
sine qua non, its very essence, lies in the individual's ability, and
need, to isolate for feeling and contemplation the relation 'I:
World.'"

That, in fact, is the begin-all-end-all business of the poet's life. It is the
most private and precious, as it is also the most primitive, of adventures,
the adventure which underlies all others: for until he knows himself, and
his twinned worlds, the inner and outer, how can he possibly know the
worlds, inner or outer, of another? (CC, 98)

"Changing Mind" is Aiken's supremely "inner poem." The full
impact of its exploration of the relation "I: World" is clear beyond a
doubt in its last sections:

   Doctor Wundt, grown taller, and my father,
Flinging one haloed image on the stream,

Sang, with one voice, a mournful requiem.
"Inheritor!" This was the word they said,
But also sang, "Alas, Narcissus dead,
Narcissus daily dead, that we may live!"

4

My father which art in earth
From whom I got my birth,
What is it that I inherit?
From the bones fallen apart
And the deciphered heart,
Body and spirit.

My mother which art in tomb
Who carriedst me in thy womb,
What is it that I inherit?
From the thought come to dust
And the remembered lust,
Body and spirit.

Father and mother, who gave
Life, love, and now the grave,
What is it that I can be?
Nothing but what lies here,
The hand still, the brain sere,
Naught lives in thee

Nor ever will live, save
It have within this grave
Roots in the mingled heart. . . .

(SP, 77-78)

The power, of course, is not in the stark simplicity of the message of the speaker's connection—for good and ill—with mother and father, a fact of existence shared by all.5 Nor is it even in the shocking realization that destruction and creation of self are united in the artist's sacrifice that others may live in his art. It is in the reader's being made to share these psychological revelations as he struggles for coherence and understanding, plunging in and through the perceptual confusions of the poem. "One of the responsibilities of a writer," Aiken said in an interview, "[is] that he should take off the mask" (PR, 118). In "Changing Mind," Aiken has taken it off in layers, and during our participation in the physical and psychic incoherences of the poem we have discovered ourselves as part of that unlayering. "What I had in mind," Aiken wrote of another poem, in words that might well have been explaining "Changing Mind,"

is an increased awareness at all costs even if it involves continuing fragmentation of the world within the world without, and even if it involves the risk of disintegration of the ego. The poet must be capable of doing this: it's his job. (Shenandoah, 34)

In "Changing Mind" Conrad Aiken did his "job" well. His examination in "The Coming Forth by Day of Osiris Jones" of perception and the human consciousness from the focus of an individual's "outer" world is no less effective.

In March 1931 Aiken wrote to Robert Linscott, explaining "Osiris Jones" and complaining a bit about his friend's unresponsiveness to its innovations:

Osiris? . . . You object to its stenographic nature—but that, my dear fellow, is what was aimed at. This is a behaviourist drama. Everything, almost, is reported scientifically and in brief notes from outside. Character or identity is reduced to nothing but a series of reflected items. Jones becomes the statements of various people, the rooms he lived in, the signs he read, a moment of awareness when facing a mirror. . . . A story? My god. What do I want with a story? . . . The very essence of the thing is that there should be no story. (SL, 171)

Instead of a story, Aiken presents a catalogue: a series of lists of names, places, objects, memories, snatches of conversation, public and private utterances in many voices, all assembled as if to test a theory that the best way to take the measure of a man is quite literally with scales, calipers, pens and pencils, rulers, record books. The poem's headnotes themselves suggest that when the assemblage of bones, flesh, and blood that was named Peter Jones "comes forth" after death, he will be trailing the muck and clutter of a lifelong accumulation of peripheral concerns, things, people, happenings: Peter Jones equals "The Things," "The Costumes," "Characteristic Comments," "Inscriptions in Sundry Places," "Various Rooms," "Unofficial Report Made by Divers Trysting Places," "Report Made by a Medical Student to Whom Was Assigned for Inspection the Case of Mr. Jones," "Speeches Made by Books, Stars, Things and People."

Perhaps Jones *is* more than these, the whole more than the sum of the parts. But questions concerning the nature of meaning seem precisely to be Aiken's meaning. As Aiken explained why Jones is called Osiris:

As regards my title, I can do no better than quote "The Book of the Dead," page 29: "In all the copies of 'The Book of the Dead' the deceased is always called 'Osiris,' and as it was always assumed that those for whom they were written would be found innocent when weighed in the Great Balance, the words 'true of voice' which were equivalent in meaning to 'innocent and acquitted,' were always written after their names."[6]

And, indeed, Mr. Jones assures his reflected image that he is more than a disparate assemblage of parts slipping past one another:

I am a mind
whose wanderings
are unconfined
north south and east
and west I go. . . . .
          (SP, 94)

Too, E. A. Wallis Budge—whose British Museum pamphlet, *The Book of the Dead,* provided Aiken his primary source for the poem—describes the Egyptian notion of the buried man in terms suggesting that within the body lies a kernel of true being that must be comprehended and protected.

Thus, as we have seen, the whole man consisted of a natural body, a spiritual body, a heart, a double, a soul, a shadow, an intangible ethereal casing or spirit, a form, and a name. All these were, however, bound together inseparably, and the welfare of any single one of them concerned the welfare of all. For the well-being of the spiritual parts it was necessary to preserve from decay the natural body. . . .

The texts are silent as to the time when the immortal part began its beatified existence; but it is probable that the Osiris of a man only attained to the full enjoyment of spiritual happiness after the funeral ceremonies had been duly performed and the ritual recited.[7]

But in Aiken's poem, the disparities between one appearance and another, and between all appearances and how things might be within, constitute the recited ritual.

"The Osiris," Budge wrote, "consisted of all the spiritual parts of a man gathered together in a form which resembled him exactly."[8] And yet the Osiris of Peter Jones, resembling nothing so exactly as a name plus an empty space, has no shape other than the forms passing through it, even though these represent facts as autobiographical as any in Aiken's poetry.

I don't think there is any detail in it that hasn't immediate reference to myself in one way or another. And more than that, the medical report which forms one section of it was actually a medical report made by my father when he was an interne at Harvard Medical School. (BBC II, 4)

It is as if Aiken has chosen to fully test his insights into the nature of human perception by deliberately using his own most intimate facts. To observe external details, even (perhaps especially) the most familiar ones, is not sufficient for a genuine understanding of a life. Because of the ways this poem of surfaces keeps us distant from any involvement or concern with the characters or happenings, we find ourselves comprehending not the central figure Jones so much as our own perceptual formulae and the tricks and turns Aiken used in putting his piece together.

If a poem is, as William Carlos Williams once suggested, "a small (or large) machine made of words,"[9] then this is a poem in which the creakings of the machine and our response to seeing the exposed gears are in large part the subject. We learn a good deal about what we have read, what our sense of language is, and

what we expect from a story. We appreciate the poem for the
ways it enables us to preen and strut *our* "knowing" and fills us
with self-congratulation about how much we see of the poet's literary allusions, sources, and word play. It is good fun, but
Aiken's joke is on us: we think we are making meaning ade-
quately simply by referring "objective" details to established categories of information.

The poem gives us information aplenty. "Remarks on the Person of Mr. Jones" (SP, 85)—early and late—tell us the
incontrovertible "facts" of a life:

The trained nurse
     it's a fine boy, not a blemish, God bless him
                                        (SP,85)

The face
     mmmmmmmmm . . . mmmmmm
                              (SP, 83)

Facies
     sallow and somewhat haggard; thin and pallid;
     . . . .
     The eyes are sunken, broad dark rings around them;
     conjunctivae, pale; gums, not affected;
     no blue line, and no sponginess. Tongue-moist.
                                        (SP, 99)

Extremities
     forearms and thighs, dotted with small spots—
     average about a pinhead size (some larger)—
     varying from the color of fresh blood
     to almost black. Are not removed by pressure,—
     not raised above the surface, sharply outlined:
     . . . .
     The skin, harsh, scaly. Follicles, not prominent.
     Muscles, somewhat flaccid.
                                        (SP, 100)

From unblemished to blemished: the poem presents a defusing of the emotional and philosophic possibilities inherent in the acts of birth and death. The eyes see a great deal of the minute particulars but record neither a sense of being nor of becoming—or even of having been. The details, peculiarly neutralized, appear without any attention to progression of effect because, clearly, in the logic of the scientific laboratory all parts of the specimen are equally useful and important.

Yet the poem *is* energized, full of the life of language and creative play that is most unscientific, and it is here that Aiken tricks us. The percipient being of the poem, in motion all the time, is the poet himself. Outrageous puns and wildly incongruous literary allusions lace the poem, delighting the reader who places them but who, having done so, knows no more about where he is, or why, or where he is going, than before. It is a poetic game of let's see what we can see, and having seen it, let's see if it's anything at all.

While pendulums complain—"Pain-pang-pain-pang-pain-pang" (SP, 103)—echoes of Poe mixed with Freud sounding in our heads, and the beds cry out with Hamlet's voice for the world to notice the "Foul enseamèd sheets" (SP, 104),[10] the coffin speaks the horrendous pun, "I also serve who only lie in wait" (SP, 84), and the snow falls with a shivering sigh from Lear's fool to tell us, "Poor Pete's a-cold" (SP, 107). We cannot help catching the allusions and unraveling the puns, and we cannot help being delighted by our ability to do so, feeling perhaps for a moment that because we can do this, we are really on our way to fully perceiving the poem. But, thinking that we are being put in touch with our living pasts through literary echoes, we find only that we have become empiricists ourselves, compiling our own list of literary data that, because it lacks context and emotive resonance, is merely an assemblage of facts to place alongside all the others. We are little more than measuring devices, not unlike the pendulum, the ruler, or the thermometer. It is a good trick, but one that has the serious result of making us pause to consider our systems of learning and knowing. When one accepts the premise that it is possible and worthwhile to examine human nature while situated as an outside observer—measuring and recording the facts of a man but refusing to be a man for fear of losing "objectivity" in involvement—one discovers that both thing observed and observer are diminished.[11] It is not, finally, a laughing matter.

As for making sure that we can recognize the poem's internal structures and data as well as its external references, Aiken ritualizes his descriptions so that we are sure to recognize repetitions. We store the information, such as it is, until with a twist the pattern of accumulated knowledge is altered. Thus we hear the red-haired Jones described early and often as "bricktop." The repeated tag seems offered to give us a sense of the man's physical presence. Yet this descriptive purpose is undercut when we find ourselves near the end of the poem confronting a haunted house (perhaps a symbol of the empty moments of Jones's life, or more literally the place he lived, now vacant) which announces with ironic reverberations that ripple down the length of the poem: "I knew it—that brick at the top is loose" (SP, 112). It's a solid joke, though, full of innuendo about Jones's sanity, about the solidity of this poem, especially about the worth of our own "seeing" thus far—the worth of our seeming to have recognized essential details of the person and of the building blocks of poetic structures.

The poetic play is continuous, and manipulation of the reader is unceasing. Perhaps the most telling of the lists of recognitions is the one that includes different dictions and that hints at the variety of ways our language can be used to communicate denotative and connotative meanings:

[the poetic alliterative:] "this is a roiled reflection of the face"
                                                              (SP, 86)

[the elevated Biblical:] "let him go forth into the field of flowers
                        let him go forth into the field of offerings
                        let him go forth into the field of reeds."
                                                              (SP, 108)

[the mythopoeic:] "so the three caravels to westward veiling
                  foamworthy . . . seething
                  southward in soft atlantic saw you sinking"
                                                              (SP, 91-92)

[street slang:] "He'd steal a penny from a dead man's eye"
(SP, 104)

"well, he's a good egg, at that"
(SP, 106)

[medical jargon:] "Supra-clavicular (and infra-clavicular) regions
no more depressed than anaemia warrants.
. . . Apex beat not seen."
(SP, 99)

In its way, the poem presents not so much a coherent aesthetic formulation as an encyclopedia of perceptual possibilities.

While Aiken has not here enabled us to see the Osiris of Peter Jones in the traditional sense of spiritual wholeness, he *has* offered a lesson on some aspects of the ways in which a world is perceived, and he has also managed to present, if not a simple coherent view of one man, a kind of popular culture picture of an age. This picture is seen in the objects that clutter the interiors of the poem's places: "*Kitchen* / tin mug of coffee on an oilcloth table; / advertisements of pills for female ills" (SP, 91); in the scribblings on the walls of the public lavatory: "Mable Waters 26 John Street / . . . / it was down in the Lehigh Valley—me and my saucy Sue" (SP, 89); in the signs on subway walls: "the cough and sneeze / both spread disease" (SP, 88); and in the inscriptions on billboards, streetcars, and vending machines: "smoke Sweet Caporals," "do not speak to the motorman," "insert one cent then press the rod / push push push push" (SP, 87).

"The Forerunner and Firebringer": Coda

Hugh Kenner once called T. S. Eliot an "Invisible Poet," systematically anonymous, full of literary camouflage.[12] As Jonathan Holden has suggested recently, this is an attitude that seems often to define the full sweep of modern poetry itself. Modernism "has . . . come to denote a poetic based roughly on the position Eliot outlined in 'Tradition and the Individual Talent': a poetic that

involves 'extinction of the personality' so that in most of the
famous modernist poems the poet's personality and presence is
so peripheral as to be scarcely noticeable."[13] Conrad Aiken, too,
decided early that "his life must be lived *offstage,* behind the
scenes, out of view" (U, 165); and he was as firmly committed as
his friend to the

> persistent belief that form must be form, that inventions of form must
> keep a basis in order and tradition, that a mere surrender to the pleasure
> . . . of chain making in the bright colors of the colloquial and the collo-
> quial cadence was not enough, not a substitute for the dark and difficult
> and, yes, painful process of cryptopoiesis, and that this, in turn, must,
> like a compass, have its true North in the shape of a conscious and artic-
> ulated *Weltanschauung,* a consistent view. (U, 219)

Yet Aiken chose as complete a visibility as he could within the
framework of his well-formed art itself. For Aiken believed further, with Henry James, that the most profound quality of an art-
work will always be the quality of the mind of its producer.[14] The
"mind" for Aiken meant full "consciousness," whereas the poem
was the arena where the poet's, the reader's, and by implication,
the world's awareness engaged in an adventure of mutual discoveries.

> Poetry . . . must think: it must embody the full consciousness of man at
> that given moment. It can not afford to lag behind the explorations of
> knowledge, whether of the inner or outer worlds: these it is its business
> to absorb and transmute. What made Elizabethan poetry great, above
> all, was the fearlessness with which it plunged into the problem of con-
> sciousness itself. No item of man's awareness was too trivial to be noted,
> too terrifying to be plumbed. . . . In all this I am not so much suggest-
> ing that poets should be philosophers as that—in the sense of being ques-
> tioners and understanders—they should be philosophic. The good poet
> must have not merely the clearest and subtlest of sensibilities; he must
> have also the boldest and subtlest of minds. The poet who is a mere drift-
> ing sensorium in a world of sense is of no more use to us than the most
> word-chopping of logicians. Each of them can afford us pleasure at par-
> ticular moments only. (CC, 80-81)

For Aiken, as for few other poets of our time, the "articulated" and "consistent view" paradoxically demanded acceptance of the idea of change at the center of things.

> The consistent view had shaped itself slowly and intermittently out of the incredibly rich pour of new discoveries, new ideas, the miraculously rapid expansion of man's knowledge inward and outward. . . . *Gnowthi seauton*—that was still the theme . . . and now at last the road was being opened for the only religion that was any longer tenable or viable, a poetic comprehension of man's portion in the universe, and of his potentialities as a poietic shaper of his own destiny, through self-knowledge and love. The final phase of evolution of man's mind itself to ever more inclusive consciousness: in that, and that alone, would he find the solvent of all things. (U, 219-20)

In his first decades as a writer Conrad Aiken discovered self and form, psychology and technique. The continual explorations and experiments with modes of seeing and knowing, which often compelled his readers' participation, enabled him to take a giant step toward fulfilling the poet's function, as he explained to John Gould Fletcher in 1946: "I see him as the . . . forerunner, fire-bringer, orderer and releaser; the one who by finding the word for life makes life possible and coherent, and puts it within the reach of all" (SL, 270). "It is only the poet," he wrote, "who by adding the feelings, or rather by transmuting his knowledge *through* the feelings, makes, at each stage of man's development, the *whole* statement; he always has the last word, because it is always the first—the poet was and is the one who invents language. Which is tantamount to inventing experience, or awareness" (SL, 270-71).

6 Absolute Fiction and Beyond

Blue Voyage, Great Circle, King Coffin

Between 1927 and 1940 Aiken published five novels. The first three, *Blue Voyage* (1927), *Great Circle* (1933), and *King Coffin* (1935), sharply clarify developments in his investigations of human consciousness. Having begun to explore various perceptual vantages, examining in the process ways that the world and the individual are linked in a dance of mutual definition, Aiken struggled in the 1930s to crystallize philosophic and psychological attitudes in his two sets of "Preludes" and in "Landscape West of Eden." His work became more reflective, less playful, however serious the playing. By the end of the decade he was further broadening his scope of subject to include works dealing with the individual consciousness in relation to national and personal places and histories, works that were still concerned with modes of seeing but also with the meanings and implications of external things seen. The novels pointedly reveal the changing and changed points of focus because mimetic fictions, concerned with external persons, places, and actions in ways that lyrics often are not, enable the reader to observe the human mind dealing more concretely with "realistic" worlds. Suggesting aspects of seeing the human consciousness "in action," Aiken's first three novels provide the critic with a uniquely valuable foundation for, and complement to, comprehension of the shapes and textures of knowing prevalent in Aiken's more abstract lyrics of this remarkably productive writing period.

When, in his autobiographical essay *Ushant,* Aiken speaks of "these forms, these coagulations of light, into scenes or events, the shapes of experience, which gradually became the shape of oneself" (U, 35), he is giving us a clue to how best to approach his first novel. Like many of the poems of the twenties, it is a kind of experiment in seeing. *Blue Voyage* presents not a representation of the actual world so much as a "kind of singular abstraction and attenuated contact with the real, an 'absoluteness'" (CC, 167) such as Aiken himself discovers in the later novels of Henry James.

"There are no canons for the novel," Aiken had written in the July 1925 issue of *The Dial*. "The novelist, so long as he remains interesting, can do what he likes. . . . Whatever mode he chooses he will impregnate deeply, if he is successful, with his own character. The novel is the novelist's inordinate and copious lyric" (CC, 347). Already more than a year into the writing of *Blue Voyage*—his own fictive departure from tradition—Aiken seemed to be preparing his critics for problems to come. Despite the visible energy directed toward the creation of incident, Aiken's novel was not to be comprehended by the usual methods of considering narrative, scene, or even interaction of characters. Avowedly influenced by Joyce's *Ulysses,* yet clearly exhibiting his own voice, Aiken sought to examine not only the product of, or reasons for, individual change but also the very feeling of the experience of change.[1] At its best, this absolute fiction gives us "the effects of contrasting and conflicting tones and themes, a kind of underlying simultaneity in dissimilarity" (CC, 128). We also discover, much to our excitement and frustration, that the boundaries of the subjective and objective worlds are inevitably shifting across one another.

As we might expect from a writer who regards the novel as a modern lyric, Aiken's conception of fictive form owes a greater debt to the art of poetry than to that of storytelling. Instead of a traditional narrative technique involving patterns of sequential development, Aiken's technique is essentially an organizational method of discontinuity, of seemingly unrelated details kaleidoscopically juxtaposed for the reader to piece together. The juxtaposition creates an acute perception of the details unencumbered by confusing interrelationships; and yet we encounter at the same time a process in which the systematic meanings of the discrete details are mutually destroyed. It is a process of energy and tension out of which will emerge new meanings and new total forms.

Blue Voyage, an almost suffocatingly intense exploration of an individual consciousness, represents Aiken's most radical departure from the traditional well-plotted novel. He wrote to Robert Linscott on 28 August 1924, just as the novel got underway in earnest, "The action, I hear you cry?" And he answered his own question, "Almost none, in the accepted sense" (SL, 94). Inner worlds engulf the reader, completely determining whatever sense of external happenings he manages to get. If we think of the outer world of most novels as a kind of circle, with a primary consciousness at its center, we can say of *Blue Voyage* that the main character, Demarest, is simultaneously center and circle. It is almost as if Aiken set out to depict for his time the hypothesis of Percy Shelley, whom he studied with Santayana at Harvard and whose writing clearly influenced his own. As Shelley wrote: "Each is at once the centre and the circumference; the point to which all things are referred and the line in which all things are contained."[2]

Let us remember once again Santayana's excellent evaluation of psychology and creativity:

Our logical thoughts dominate experience only as the parallels and meridians make a checkerboard of the sea. They guide our voyage without controlling the waves, which toss for ever in spite of our ability to ride over them to our chosen ends. . . .

. . . [The poet] dips into the chaos that underlies the rational shell of the world and brings up some superfluous image, some emotion dropped by the way, and reattaches it to the present object . . . [and] he paints in again into the landscape the tints which the intellect has allowed to fade from it. If he seems sometimes to obscure a fact, it is only because he is restoring an experience.[3]

Blue Voyage, viewed by the eye at the level of the sea's surface, at the level of the novel's actions, is quite simply the tale of William Demarest's voyage from New York to England in search of his lost love. En route, he talks to one reporter, strikes up a few casual friendships, plays one game of bridge and one of chess, eats and sleeps, and experiences both rejection by the beloved of his search and the promise of a new, shipboard affair. This does not produce, however, the high-seas romance or shipboard intrigue that a reader might hope for, or expect, given the potential in the broad outlines of the story. Demarest's conscious thoughts and actions no more control *Blue Voyage* than Santayana's "parallels and meridians" control the sea. Aiken draws from the depths of Demarest's experience the words, thoughts, images, and emotions that are part of perception and presents them with a kind of swelling and contracting rhythm that makes them perceivable both individually and as interrelated parts of a whole.

Like many of the sea tales of Herman Melville, whose work Aiken admired, *Blue Voyage* begins with a scene of departure from land. And as in Melville's fictions, we step off into a watery world where the solidity of the ship is illusory. The ocean liner seems as if it should provide a circumscribed territory within which issues and relationships can be distinctly perceived and measured. But our sense of dislocation in *Blue Voyage* begins on land and expands on board ship. In fact, we have difficulty even visualizing basic physical places (cabins, smoking room, dining room, and so forth) once we have left a few familiar physical realities behind on the shoreline. Old memories are carried out to sea by Aiken's main characters, where they mingle with new thoughts, new faces, and new places half perceived and half created, dislocating the reader thoroughly.

Consider the novel's first sentence: "'Will you stop,' said William Demarest, leaning his head out of the taxi window, 'at the corner drug store?'" (BV, 17). This terse, seemingly referential beginning wrenches the reader quickly into the middle of things and promises all sorts of information to follow. Surely we are about to discover four essential facts: (1) the identity of William Demarest, (2) the destination of the taxi that displays William Demarest's head, (3) the corner, the drugstore, and the city where we are about to stop, and (4) who needs medicine—what kind and why. Such promises fulfilled are the very guts of fictional realism, after all, and at the very least they will assist us to

willingly suspend our disbelief in the fictive world we are about
to enter.

The facts are forthcoming, but not until Aiken has taken us on
a flight far from the taxi, the corner, and the drugstore and has
lodged us—even while giving us some of the facts by implication—in the terrain of a dream, or myth, or mindscape.

It had suddenly occurred to him that he had forgotten his sea-sick
pills—the little pink and green box was indispensable. . . . A charm
against sea serpents. As he stood on the marble floor, amid the thousand
bottles and vials and jars . . . the sound of the approaching voyage came
loudly about him. Waves crashing against black portholes. . . . Bugles
blowing in sour corridors—red-carpeted corridors which suddenly,
unaccountably, became hills to climb. . . . And the ship. . . . A con-
gregation of gigantic mushroomlike ventilators, red-throated, all belch-
ing a smell of hot oil and degenerate soup, with sounds of faint
submarine clankings. Among them, a few pale stewards, faces like cau-
liflowers, carrying gladstone bags and hot-water bottles ... He suddenly
felt queasy. (BV, 17)

But before we can orient ourselves to this fairy-tale landscape of
sea serpents, giant vegetable ventilators, dragonlike ships, and
cauliflower faces, we are back in the city, with a street finally identified in such a way as to begin to fulfill the simple promise of our
opening: "in the taxi . . . they passed through Twenty-third
Street" (BV, 17). Of course we have already received information
about such things as the reasons for the drug stop (seasick pills)
and the taxi's probable destination (the docks of New York City),
but we received it only in passing, amidst an assemblage of details
that confused our sense of place. Now, barely have we registered
the idea of being on Twenty-third Street, New York City, the
United States of America, when we are in flight once more—first
absorbing more information about place while disregarding
boundaries of time, then arriving temporally confused at a dock
that is not a dock, to board a ship that is something other, for a
voyage not to England but "into the infinite."

As they passed . . . he lost fifteen years of his life . . . and caught sight of
himself (a very pale, sober-looking young man) mounting the stone

steps of No. 421. The shy young widow was sitting in the garden. . . .
How had she managed to conceal so long from him, in their meetings in
hall or on stairs, that she had only one hand? ... And Stedman. . . . And
the bedbugs . . . labeled, *"Take one before retiring. Dr. Stedman."* . . .
The old painter was dead. What had become of the detective? ... and his
thin submissive little wife. . . .
    "Here you are sir!" . . .
    And there he was. The wharf. An enormous . . . place, cavernous,
engulfing bales and trunks. . . . Where should he enter? The usual terror assailed him. . . . He carried his bag into the great sounding gloom
. . . with its smells of oakum and hemp and slimy piles . . . dodged his
way among thumping trucks . . . everywhere, each pushed by a pirate;
and at last, through a great sea door, caught sight of the black iron side
of the vessel. . . . What disgusting animals ships were! always fouling
their sides with garbage . . . . O Thalassa! Thalassa! Unmerciful sea.
He was already fairly launched into the infinite, the immense solitude. . . . Yes: alone. Alone with the sea for eight days: alone in a cage
with a world of tigers roaring outside. (BV, 17-18)

We are not permitted to substitute expected perceptions for a
perception of the details themselves. Indeed, the "facts" are mis-
leading to the reader trying to piece a plot together. Neither Stedman, the widow, the painter, nor the detective and wife reappear
in the novel. But snatches of scenes in Demarest's past, momen-
tarily remembered voices, together with fractured glimpses of the
present, disjointed visions of space and time, continue to jostle
one another—and always for the same purpose: not to explore
the world we see before us but to take us into disturbing places
behind the eye.
    The method of presentation we encounter in the novel's first
few pages continues to determine the shape of the whole.
Throughout, a few sharp facts serve as anchors for a looping,
wavelike motion of accumulating details. Material gathers, falls
back to touch on a particular fact, explaining a bit more of it each
time, then moves off to more distant chaotic material, falling
back to a particular fact once more, now with a larger, massing
wavelike motion. Thus at the start we do come to realize that
Demarest is leaving New York, where he has lived on and off for
some time, and more important we realize that he carries with
him as he travels the chimeras he is trying to outdistance.

Finally, we recognize that each broad unit of wavelike motion relates to other broad units of motion occurring later on. These "waves" of confusing information do not constitute a forward motion in the novel, but when seen side by side, like so many of the smaller particles of each wave, they help to explain each other. Thoughts, moods, and speculations of one unit become overtones that help us perceive the state of mind represented in the next unit. It is an inward journey, not a progression, that we are experiencing.

The "facts" never become for the reader much more than points of reference in a sea of psychic turbulence, but gradually their significance in terms of Demarest's psychic ramblings become more comprehensible. Amidst the flux, some narrative units stand out and may be usefully considered. Observe, then, three mental episodes—juxtapositions of fragments that together produce a new configuration suggesting Demarest's self-loathing and his confused attitudes about love and lust, innocence and experience, childhood and adulthood. In each fragment, images of the present moment are placed side by side with memories and nightmares. The promise of a healthy love affair with a fresh and appealing young Irish girl breeds, in the strange recesses of the mind, recollections of an innocent toy fire engine whose smoke suddenly turns out to hide scenes of juvenile sexual corruption. Impressions of the rhythm of ship, wind, and sea sounds are radically transformed into thoughts of moans of lust, rhythms of swarms of insects—maggots, gnats, locusts—and sounds of time ticking away into a sick and empty future of lost innocence. And throughout the fragments, the repeated image of the child Demarest as Caligula—the monster who manipulated for personal gain the public memory of his grandparents and parents and who Suetonius tells us committed incest with each of his three sisters—gathers to cast light on the theme of Demarest's sexual confusion. It reveals his sense of moral bankruptcy, especially as it relates to his ambivalent attitude toward love and hate of his dead parents, whose murder-suicide he discovered.[4]

Little Caligula ran on the sidewalk, pulling after him a toy fire engine, from which poured the thick smoke of burning excelsior. Little Caligula invited Gladys Dyson to come to the vacant lot. . . . Walking . . . saw a Negro and Negress embracing, heard the Negress moan. . . . How had [beauty] so managed to complicate itself with evil and sensuality and the danks and darks of sex?—It had come in . . . with the seven-year locust. . . . Caligula . . . beseeches you to be kind to him. . . . The Irish girl in the next room again moved the bed curtains, brass rings on brass rod—Zring. (BV, 64-65)

Zring, went the Irish girl's bed curtains . . . and then the bunk creaked . . . and an elbow thumped the matchboard partition close to Demarest's ear, and then grazingly bruised it again, and then a padded round knee bumped, and the elbow again more softly knocked ... Who's there, i' the name of the devil? . . . Knock again. . . . Is it you, darling? In the dark? where? Listen to the wind moaning. . . . Listen to the sea. . . . We are silences drowned in an abyss of sound. The ship is sinking. The world is sinking. God is sinking. . . . Now,—in the open sore of space,—the mortal son and the daughter immoral, make of the world their trysting place. . . . Swarms. . . . the maggot . . . quarries in the very pulse of love. . . . This was where Goya lived: in Portobello Road. . . . *Goya saw the Great Slut pick The chirping human puppets up. And laugh, with pendulous mountain lip, And drown them.* . . . *Or squeeze their little juices out In arid hands.* . . . *He* HEARD *the* SECONDS IN *his* CLOCK CRACK *like* SEEDS, DIVULGE *and* POUR ABYS*mal* FILTH *of* NO*thing*NESS BETWEEN *the* PEN*dulum* AND *the* FLOOR. . . . MISERY. Say it savagely . . . the same . . . rhythm as that of King Caligula. . . . I have sinned; but I have paid the price. My father was cruel. (BV, 72-75)

We may go on thinking, remembering, in a confused sort of way—a jumble of sensations. Or rarefied—a tiny gnat song of consciousness ... Dr. Kiernan stated that when he called in at 7.13 there was still a spark of life ... she looked alive but extraordinarily still. Eyes shut. Mouth wide open, fixed in the act of screaming, but silent. TERROR! ... Perhaps she knew I was there, looking at her, and then walking softly, quickly, away. . . . "Yes, William, I am dead. But I know you are there. Do you want to know if an accident has occurred? Yes. A dreadful accident. . . . I am quite all right, now. Run and wake Nanny. Shut the door into the nursery. Wind the clocks on Sunday morning. And say good-by to this house and world forever ..." . . . Do you hear me, Cynthia? . . . Forgive me! Absolve me! Let me bury my infant's face against you and weep! . . . The crying child. . . . Our father that weepest in heaven. . . . My father, which art in earth. Billy who was tied to the bedpost and beaten. . . . The crying child will find his adored blue shawl. . . . Ah Psyche from the regions whish. . . . Her scarf blew away along the deck and I ran after

it. The squall blew her skirt up. . . . They laughed. In my left ear my
heart *te thrum te thrum.* The Sea. Sea. Sea. Sea. (BV, 100, 103-5)

What a jarring mix of communicative possibilities Aiken gives
us: flashes of naturalistic detail—a congress of sights and stinks
that immediately evoke a multiplicity of times, places, and circumstances. There are glimpses of Punch and Judy, Shakespeare,
and the Bible, wrenched into alien contexts. The visual nightmares of an artist are suggested—Goya or hints of Bosch invoked
at least indirectly. Often places, while felt strongly, dissolve in our
grasp even as we make contact. Portobello road becomes anywhere, then nowhere. A crying child on shipboard mingles his
shrieks with the cries of the child Demarest remembers in specific
yet strangely unspecified ways, the child that we assume is young
Demarest himself. And the sorrowful sound merges with the
silent (and sometimes not so silent) keening of the adult
Demarest, who longs for love and sleep. The child's cry, finally a
voice without a specific source, spreads out to fill up all of time
and space, remembered and to come, with a message of misery.
Ideas like love, fear, and guilt give up their meanings slowly, by
way of shimmering implications rather than through direct communication. The final impression is one of scenes perceived with
a soft and shifting focus: the adult's perspective, rational yet
often confused, superimposed on a world glimpsed with a child's
eye, slightly illogical, full of mistaken proportions.

It seems that every conceivable kind of creative imagining is
employed for the final effect.[5] Within the clouded whole, some
things are made to seem especially vivid, as the imagination acts
upon its object by particularizing it and intensifying it (the child's
fire engine, the discovery of the mother's body). Some episodes
are presented so that we perceive the imagination as distancing
and stylizing its object (the response to the Irish girl with its theatrical language and rhythm). Archetypal imagining is strongly
felt in parts of the treatment of the Caligula and Goya episodes.
And over all we can feel strongly the working of a compositive
imagination blending disparate elements with such effectiveness
that we are made to think of Samuel Coleridge's account of

esemplastic activity. Here the poet "described in ideal perfection" writes, "diffus[ing] a tone and spirit of unity, that blends, and (as it were) fuses, each into each, by that synthetic and magical power, to which we have exclusively appropriated the name of imagination."[6]

The overview that emerges from our perceiving these episodes alongside each other is something like a reverse of the configuration that occurs when a stone is dropped in still water. We discover circle inside circle. At the outmost circumference of these inward-spiraling circles we find the "events" of both Demarest's failed pursuit of Cynthia and of his speculated pursuit of the Irish girl (or later of Faubion, another potential shipboard romance). Inside this circle is Demarest the little lost boy discovering life without adult guidance. The next circle contains Demarest the father-hater; then Demarest facing the trauma of finding his mother's corpse. From the widest circle to the narrowest, we find a single emotion and behavior pattern: guilt and a resulting incapacity for action. The innermost circle explains the source of it. Demarest is, in effect, a man traumatized at an early age, seeking not so much a mature relationship as a combination of punishment and solace.

Offered the possibilities of acceptance or sublimation, Demarest finds it difficult to get beyond the latter. Of his original plan for the novel Aiken wrote: "The intention is primarily . . . to present . . . Demarest's own particular psychological problem *indirectly* . . . his struggle for balance as between Cynthia and Faubion, the former being a symbol of adolescent sublimation and refusal, the latter a symbol of maturity and acceptance. . . . The end? Cynthia cuts him dead, and he refuses Faubion . . . and rides . . . to London with Silberstein, swapping lubricious recollections. He is now an adult, but profoundly unhappy" (SL, 93-94). The published ending, while not so negative, still leaves us with a question about Demarest's ability to act, as it is Faubion who seeks *him* out in the last sentences of the novel, thus qualifying what might otherwise seem a depiction of the beginnings of Demarest's psychological growth.

The lack of conclusiveness at the novel's end, while it may be

frustrating to our Hollywood instincts, is aesthetically sound.
The pieces that the reader has gradually assembled, commenting
on each other as they do, enable us to understand Demarest's private hell without suggesting facilely how he might help himself.
Little Caligula, just discovering the tortuous beginnings of sexu-
ality, and little Billy, just discovering the terrible endings of it, are
superimposed on the adult Demarest's imaginings of sex. Aiken
thus presents a vision of the attraction to, yet horror of, sexual
acceptance that clearly stands in the way of Demarest's quest for
completion. The reader's perception of Demarest, like his comprehension of the novel as a whole, is one in which cause and
effect, seen piecemeal, seem bound irrevocably together. Demarest seems to exist in a kind of continuing past-present, in which
every instant is marked by the intrusion of memory constantly
changing the reality of time and place. We cannot prescribe a cure
for Demarest's problems because we cannot even share a point of
vantage. The English philosopher F. H. Bradley, who so influenced Aiken's friend and fellow poet T. S. Eliot, wrote: "all that
we suffer, do and are forms one psychical totality . . . experienced all together as a coexisting mass, not perceived as parted
and joined even by relations of coexistence."[7] It seems a view
applicable to Aiken's first novel. *Blue Voyage,* while giving us no
"conclusions," has vividly demonstrated the interconnectedness
of subject and object, thing perceived and perceiver. Demarest,
revealing his creator's own goals and problems as a writer,
laments the difficulties of "embroil[ing himself] in complications
. . . qualifications and relativities."

I must always wrap it up in tissue upon tissue of proviso and aspect . . .
turn . . . each side to the light; producing in the end not so much a uni-
tary work of art as . . . a phantasmagoric world of disordered colors and
sounds . . . perceptible only in terms of . . . the fragmentary. . . . I have
deliberately aimed at this effect, in the belief that the old unities and simplicities will no longer serve. No longer serve, I mean, if one is trying to
translate, in any form of literary art, the consciousness of modern man.
And this is what I *have* tried to do. I am no longer foolish enough to
think I have succeeded. (BV, 153)

Aiken himself had no need for apology. He charted his course for fiction writing in a territory beyond the secure borders of the frontier of traditional fiction as storytelling. His next novels would continue to explore that territory.

A few years after the publication of *Blue Voyage*, Aiken wrote to a friend about his next novel in progress, already more than twenty thousand words long. The work that would become *Great Circle* clearly springs from the same artistic principles and goals as the earlier novel, yet explores not simply an interior world, but the twin inner and outer worlds of its central character. *Great Circle* focuses more broadly on a self and its relationship to persons and places that partly determine the shape of self. "It's psychoanalytic in form," Aiken wrote, "and it's a damned good form. . . . [T]he question and answer gives one an ideal contrapuntal medium—if only one can manage it, keep it from clotting and slowing down" (WU, 1 June 1931). Eight months later, in January 1932, Aiken was confident that he had, in fact, kept the work from "clotting," combining the "absoluteness" of evocative yet abstract music with the speed of a tale told:

The plan has altered, as I hoped it would with a period of quiet time-maturing. . . . It will not, I think, be as "rich"—?—as B?V?. But as against that, I hope it will have a speed—or tension. . . . I may be wrong. For certainly chapter two, of which I've done 45 pages, is as expansive as anything in B.V.,—the difference being that it *drives* much harder. The . . . plan . . . the form—pleases me very much—it's one more symphony . . . I mean, it has a sort of absoluteness; without which, of course, I wouldn't know how to write a novel at all. For me, it must have that or nothing. (WU, 19 January 1932)

To an extent, Aiken continues to employ the techniques of dislocation and juxtaposition that permit the reader to focus on the nature of a distinct central consciousness without distracting considerations of how environment affects the self. But he succeeds nonetheless in presenting a fiction in which there is a discernible action and in which self is seen existing in relation to other selves and in relation to the external places that constitute an important part of any person's experience. The pieces we assemble now include not only very particularized bits of action, thought, and emotion but also large blocks of events set side by side. The suffocating closeness of *Blue Voyage* is somewhat relieved, as we are granted sufficient distance from the central consciousness of the work to perceive that in *Great Circle* things do happen. Without abandoning the technical innovations of his first novel, Aiken takes a large step toward integrating his new lyrical novel with more traditional forms of fiction.

An important clue to how to read *Great Circle* may be found in letters that Aiken wrote to Robert Linscott in 1932. On 24 November he asked his friend "if the whole is clear enough in your mind, what do you think of transposing parts two and three, so that the childhood section would follow immediately on Andy's betrayal?" (WU). Less than a month later he wrote again: "Dear Linsk . . . on the strength of your agreement with my notion of transposing parts two and three I've cabled instructions to Max [Perkins, editor of Charles Scribner's Sons]. So now it's done" (WU, 16 December 1932). Aiken, then, severely dislocates the narrative thread. Between the chaotic first chapter, dealing with his narrator's discovery of his wife's adultery (and his confrontation of her and her lover with the facts), and the almost surrealistic third and fourth chapters, in which the narrator wrestles with the implications of his situation, Aiken wedges another chapter—a strangely complete, consciously calm (albeit sometimes confused) childhood story. This large block of narrative incident serves as a reference point for our comprehension of the chapters on either side of it.

The novel opens with a lurch, as we immediately encounter a world that seems to have come unhinged. Aiken carefully delineates real physical boundaries, giving us a firm notion of where we are (the New York to Boston train) and where we are going (Andrew Cather's flat in Shepard Hall, Shepard Street, Cambridge) and why ("Fred's letter. My dear Andy, it's none of my business. . . . Bertha with Tom. . . . Treason. Horror" [GC, 173-74]). And yet the "place" won't seem to stand still: "Hurry—hurry—hurry—everything was hurrying. The train was hurrying. The world was hurrying. The landscape was hurrying. The wheels rushed blindly over the rails . . . the joints . . . the

switches: tat-te-tat-tetattle-te-tat-te-tump-te-tattle-te-tee. . . .
Birds darted in clouds" (GC, 170). At a stroke we are both located
and dislocated as our eye is led on a chase through the domain of
"the demon fireman," "the Prince of Wales," "the Maroons" and
"the Bruins," "Krazy Kat," "Pocahontas," and "the pale girl in
green satin" who rides the train beside Cather (GC, 172-75). It is a
maddening swirl reminiscent of *Blue Voyage,* but the fragments
of experience we piece together have been presented here with a
firm fictive purpose: we are being whirled into one man's consciousness where boundaries of space and time seem not to apply,
where chance associations call up more than sequential happenings do. But more immediately, we are also being whirled toward
an event—Andrew Cather's confrontation with Bertha and Tom.

Time is the enemy in this chapter, rushing Cather frighteningly
toward what seems to be an inevitable moment that he wants
both to embrace and shun. Yet the flurry offers some solace as
well: the reassurance of movement toward conclusion and a pace
of emotions that permits him to avoid real comprehension of his
own responsibility for Bertha's infidelity. The final approach to
the apartment comes with an almost excruciatingly painful accel-
eration of mental pace, as Aiken describes the final instants:

Blood was in his face, his neck and throat felt swollen and vague, everything was dimmed and rushed and whirling. . . . The red bricks glis-
tened darkly, became near and important and highly organized, rich
patterned symbol of the complicated world. Speed must replace
thought. Action must replace idea. . . . Hurry—hurry—hurry—everything was hurrying. The world was hurrying. The pain was hurrying.
The water in the gutter was hurrying. (GC, 187)

There is no hurrying the painful confrontation scene itself,
however (see GC, 190-96). The chaotic energy that was part of the
whirl of pre-encounter anger and fear is missing from the
description of the actual event. Such energy belongs more to the
shadowy realm of the partially understood preconscious than to
the domain of concrete activity with its carefully defined behavioral rules. And yet, finally, the scene reveals a confusion below

the surface of things that is the fullest in the novel thus far, as event drifts into dream at the chapter's end. Dislocation is so profound that even Andy Cather seems to have stepped outside himself, with his own disembodied spirit observing the machinery of his body and soul. Although Aiken seems to suggest that Andy's problems are all tied up with childhood, all we can ascertain for sure is that our journey, which began simply enough as a train ride from New York to Boston, has taken us not only to Shepard Street, Cambridge, but beyond into the seemingly boundless expanses of myth and mindscape.

He stared at his reflection in the greenish mirror . . . and saw his face beginning to cry. The mouth curled itself grotesquely, like a child's, like the wound in a tragic mask, his eyes closed themselves to slits, the white face began absurdly jiggling up and down. . . . He turned on the two taps . . . to drown out the extraordinary noise Andrew Cather had begun to make. A sound like a swift departure of wings, pigeon's wings, whe-whe-whe-whe-whe-whe-whe-whe . . . another hissing flight of wingbeats, and a long ooooooooooooooo. . . . Is that you, One-eye Cather?. . . If, the last time your mother spanked you . . . you refused to cry, why cry now?. . . Disgusting. Step up, ladies and gents, and see the weeping pig: the pig with wings, the pig with a glass eye. (GC, 196)

The reader picking up *Great Circle* at the second chapter, after any lapse of reading time, might well think himself beginning anew, reading a self-contained narrative of summer adventure, parental infidelity, and death, told from a child's point of view. After the kaleidoscopic beginning of the work, the cameralike objectivity with which the events of the New England summer are reported is comforting. The "facts" seem clear. We experience vividly with Andy the "smell of the pinewood walls, soaked in sea fog, but pine smelling also in the strong sunlight . . . and the wind singing through the rusty wire screens" (GC, 201). We walk with him "to the village, along the Point Road, past all the houses and windmills, the wild cherry trees and crab apples, to get the morning mail" (GC, 202). We play soldier at the Company Camp, play Indian scouting games, look idly for golf balls to sell, and gradually become attuned to the stirrings of life at the seashore. It is a calm and lovely moment in the novel, and it seems for now that even the death by drowning of Andy's mother and her lover, David, fails to interrupt the idyll for the child, and for the readers, who are compelled to see with his eyes.

————and in the playhouse that afternoon, alone, it was hot and steamy there, and quiet, and Uncle Tom came in, and looked at me . . . and I could see that he was wondering if I had been crying. But I hadn't been crying. And then he said that Sergeant Homer was at the house and wanted to ask me a few questions. . . . About how I had found the *Osprey* in the marsh channel that morning. . . .
—And you saw the tender of your uncle's boat there, in the channel, and that led to your discovery that the *Osprey* had been sunk there. . . .
—Yes, sir. . . .
—I could see some brown cloth quite close to one of the portholes, and I knew it was my mother's dress. . . .
I went out by myself to the tennis court, and met Juniper there, and he swished his tail against my bare leg and made the sound that Porper always called *puttenyarruk,* which meant that he wanted grasshoppers. . . . The tennis court was almost dry again, but the rain had made deltas in it, it would need rolling, and the lines were completely gone. It was August the 11th. . . . And would Father come down to Duxbury now—— (GC, 236-37)

Still, the very comforting, narrative simplicity of the chapter serves, finally, to dislocate the reader further. There is always a nagging frustration of not perceiving the reality of things because the child is incapable of penetrating the psychological tangle below the surface. Having already encountered the adult Andrew Cather as his life falls apart, we face the task of locating these distinct events within the mainstream of the fractured episodes we have already begun to piece together.

In fact we are in the eye of the storm. The calm orderliness of the segment makes it a reference point, still and unchanging though not completely perceived, to which we can continually turn back as we assimilate the various shifting pieces of the novel. Cather's adult story of infidelity helps us understand in retrospect the child's unstated pain that accompanies the impression of his mother's breaking marriage. These impressions in turn help us comprehend the anguish—and to some extent the source—of his adult crisis. Events outside ourselves add to and subtract from the shape of our subjective selves. Recognition of this inevitability is essential if we are to succeed in "com[ing] upward from the dark world" (GC, 282) of the imprisoning unconscious, "through the mild shafts of light . . . from plane to plane, sound to sound, meaning to meaning" (GC, 282) into consciousness.

In a sense Cather is like Demarest of *Blue Voyage,* traumatized by his early encounter with dimly apprehended complexities of adult life. Cather's partial paralysis of will and energy is the result of carrying a psychic wound—the scar of his New England summer—without comprehending and confronting it fully. This paralysis of will is at least partially responsible for pushing Bertha and her lover, Tom, together. And yet the New England summer of that last year of childhood was a time of direct connection with life as well as of sudden deprivation and disconnection from secure existence. To comprehend consciously, and thereby be reconciled to, the adult self, is to comprehend the effect of years gone by on the current moment. It is to understand, in this case, the lasting impact of both the fact of loss and of nature's vital energy immediately experienced. Such comprehension, when juxtaposed with the other slowly assembled facts and impressions of his life with Bertha and Tom, gives Cather—and the reader—the perspective necessary to understand how the "self" may thrive even though buffeted by forces beyond full control of the individual.

In two hours he would be in Duxbury. . . . Already . . . he had revisited that scene, in this week of so much revisiting—he knew it, every coarse or delicate detail of it. . . . But it would be good to touch earth. It would be good to touch, for the last time, the agony and to exorcise it . . . at last with acceptance; as one accepts such simple things as daybreak. The strange and exciting mixture of astonishment and suffering with which—at a moment of discovery—one loses oneself in order to create oneself! The end that is still conscious of its beginnings. Birth that remembers death. (GC, 295)

Aiken's third novel, *King Coffin* (1935), concludes the initial phase of his novelistic examination of human consciousness, while preparing the way for the next phase. It is Aiken's last novel to intensely explore a single self, and yet is is, finally, his first full statement of the impossibility of separating self from place and from other selves. The story is a demonstration of Aiken's conviction that failure to respond sensitively to the demands of the environment is a form of self-destruction. Ending in the suicide of would-be Nietzschean superman Jasper Ammen, it seems to present Aiken's strongest word on the theme of self-isolation.

Sentences from the first chapter, and from the last two, parenthetically enclose the interrelated thematic and technical concerns of the novel. We begin with Jasper Ammen as a god of creation "lean[ing] from the sixth floor window and project[ing] his own image upon the world" (KC, 300). He feels, we are told, "how all this scene, this width and depth of air and light, [is] becoming himself. . . . [A]nd the clear abyss of twilit sky . . . was simply his own mind" (KC, 300). And we reach conclusion with: "Lying down . . . he stared through the little square of window. . . . In mid-air, it was as if he could reverse himself . . . as if in fact he were a bird, looking in through his own window, looking . . . downward at the dark figure on the bed which was himself. . . . There was an ugly sort of distortion in it, everything was meanly and sneeringly caricatured, as by concave and convex mirrors" (KC, 399).

He opened his eyes quickly and blindly, as if to do so would stop the whirl of impressions and phrases—it was as if he were drunk, or sick, and sought any sight of the world, any fragmentary and lurching vision of a wall or ceiling, to check the wild swoop of his vertigo. (KC, 405)

The novel seems best perceived as an assemblage of visual constructions—worlds glimpsed through windows, or in mirrors, objects seen as though recorded by a camera. It is a novel of surfaces, exploring the failure of Jasper Ammen's attempts to reduce life—a threatening element as he sees it—to a form that may be controlled. From the first promise of godlike strength to the final rendering of total weakness, we are presented with variations on

a single view of Ammen's increasingly desperate attempt to stop
time and flux by forcing a pattern of his own design on the changing surface of things. The growing discrepancy between the
world Ammen insists upon perceiving and the world of things-as-
they-are marks the progress of the novel.

A contrast of mental motion and visual stasis is established
within almost the very first words of the novel. In Ammen's
world, individual—perhaps unpredictable—relationships are
reduced to sets of ideas that can be more simply dealt with. Categories of thoughts and things, then, not of human beings, sur-
round us as we are shown into the world of *King Coffin*.
Ammen's three primary human relationships are reduced to
humors, or rather ill-humors. "It was all a sort of conspiracy of
fright, with which . . . designingness and greed was mixed:
Sandbach looking for his money, Julius for his 'influence,' the
secret of his power, Gerta for his love. . . . It was necessary to be
angry . . . privately angry. Publicly . . . only the natural
expression of a natural superiority" (KC, 303-4). The relationships are seen to exist in a visually flat environment that is
completely under Ammen's perceptual control. As in a pho-
tographic essay, the physical world seems to stand still for our
gaze, whereas in the world behind the eye we move about, often
with great rapidity:

Jasper Ammen leaned from the sixth floor window. . . . Against a
streak of white light, horizontal and cold, the black tower of the ceme-
tery marked the presence, or absence, of Henry James; to the right of it,
slowly darkening, as the evening deepened to mystery, ran the irregular
line of trees toward Belmont. . . . This was all Jasper Ammen . . . it was
himself gone abroad for the greater exercise of his subtlety and
power. . . .
    . . . beyond the cement runway of the garage, a young man was sitting
in a deck chair. . . . Examined, he was at once understood. . . . To see
through him, disemboweling all his little clipped ambitions with a single
penetrating eye, was as easy as it would be, from this window, to shoot
him. . . .
    The flat roof beyond was a narrower and longer one . . . and to look at
it was to observe . . . that the cast-iron chimney pipe, at the back, had
been restored to its upright position. . . . [I]t had given him pleasure to

recognize in the street the woman who owned the house (merely by the way she walked) and to inform her (she not knowing him from Adam) that her chimney had fallen on the roof in the snow and might prove a source of danger. (KC, 300-302)

Jasper Ammen seems satisfied with the way "the value of habitual observation" (KC, 302) enables him to control his situation. And indeed, Aiken's use of fixed visual frames, which focus Jasper's more abstract thoughts for the reader, becomes a pattern of progression in the novel, as Jasper observes his world "through the wide window of the Merle" (KC, 321), contemplates "the dark pile of Beck hall" (KC, 323) from a window in Gerta's house, or watches the streets of the Boston area from various rooms, roofs, trains, and automobiles. But the more the pattern recurs, the more it seems strained; Aiken would have his reader perceive not only the way Ammen's mind and eye work together but also the fact that the "working" is a primary part of Ammen's aberration and must, finally, fail to sustain him. As the novel unfolds from one visual frame to another, the author plunges his character more fully into a world of human interaction, and it becomes increasingly clear to Aiken's readers that human beings experienced firsthand simply will not conform to being reduced or objectified as will chimneys, roofs, sunsets, or individuals contemplated from a distance in the abstract. And Ammen's frustrated response to this situation simply makes matters worse:

And especially people. Especially people. . . . They are nothing but shadows. . . .
     . . . If it was all as scattered and meaningless as that, as intangible, or almost intangible, then the only course was to extend oneself violently outward, to thrust everywhere, to occupy the world entirely with one's own entire length.... (KC, 305-6)

Ammen's sense that he is "alone and tall and superior amongst the disorderly crowd of nocturnal pedestrians" (KC, 310), that "in his own kingdom, the kingdom of thought, he could move as rapidly as he liked . . . the outside world would meanwhile stand still, and he could rejoin it whenever he wished" (KC, 310), proves false. As Ammen's camera-eyes might perceive, were they not governed by the limitations of his obsessions, the "disorderly crowd[s] of nocturnal pedestrians" are never entirely predictable. To treat them as puppets is only to discover that before long "the puppeteer [has] become subtly and dangerously entangled in the threads of his own puppets" (KC, 314)—and that, in fact, these threads are lifelines that cannot be pulled capriciously.

The central human relationship that eventually entangles Ammen is one that results from his determination to put his control of environment to a full test. He seeks to dominate not simply inanimate things, nor living beings abstracted via their reduction to the status of mental constructions. Rather he desires physical control of physical beings in his world. He determines to seek out and destroy a "complete stranger! . . . simply 'a man'" (KC, 331-32). "The terribleness of the deed must be kept pure: the problem had become a problem in art-form" (KC, 328).

There is a sublime rightness in the idea . . . it is true to yourself and to nature . . . a profound obligation if you are to become complete. . . . To injure or destroy is natural, it's life itself: to deny that is to deny life. (KC, 326)

What we encounter, however, as we observe Ammen's progress with his new "test" case—one Karl Jones, small-time advertising man—is something quite different from the purity of action entailed in formally making "art." Rather, like some sort of anti-artist, Ammen systematically de-forms Jones, first by reducing him to a visual gesture, then by defining him by the clothes he wears, and finally by one garment only. It is Ammen's way of controlling the situation: to make Jones comical is to make him manageable.

Our initial impression of Jones as simply a man on the street, recognizably normal albeit a little pathetic, rapidly gives way to a vision of Jones dehumanized, tiny, bird-furtive, and twittery:

He had come up the sloping ramp of concrete from the Arlington side, walking rather slowly, with his head a little down; he seemed to be hesitating. . . . The moment . . . passed, he gave a little cough and turned briskly. . . . He walked with an odd jauntiness, his feet turned out, and his head on one side . . . birdlike. . . . [T]he shape of his coat, which was too long for him, and had a heavy collar of cheap fur . . . accentuated this. (KC, 335-36)

The victim that Ammen stalks becomes a conglomeration of malfunctioning parts, each acting as if driven by its own abortive energy: a hand that "[goes] up. . . to touch a handhold and drop again," a "half-turned smiling face," "blue eyes behind . . . frameless spectacles . . . turned studiously downward," a "little mustache" (KC, 336). He is composed of the "essential tissue" (KC, 337) of "two suits of clothes, two pairs of shoes . . . a dirty tooth brush . . . a comb always carried in the breast pocket of the coat" (KC, 337). Or he is merely a cheap tweed hat bobbing above or below the crowd: "Ammen walked parallel with his victim: saw the grey hat appear and disappear. . . . At the corner of Bromfield . . . the tweed hat hesitated, as if about to turn to the right, but then proceeded. It crossed Tremont Street . . . sauntered slowly . . . turned once to look in at the pigeons and squirrels, but without pausing, and presently had crossed Beacon Street" (KC, 336, 338). Aiken repeatedly makes the point that the vision of Jones is Ammen's own particular view. The caricature is not offered, as it might be in a Dickens or Conrad novel, to invite the reader into a willing suspension of disbelief in which the boundary between impossible fictions and normal realities is dissolved. Ammen's view is continually juxtaposed with glimpses of a "straight" world, which serves to reinforce the sense of the normal that the reader brings to the book, contrasting Ammen's twisted perspective against reassuringly familiar streets, persons, places, and things. While Ammen continues to insist on reducing Jones's reality, Aiken is gradually building it up again in the mind's eye of his readers.

Carefully recorded commonplace details describe the environment in which Ammen pursues his animated tweed hat. The wind whirls the pages of a newspaper, and an overview of America, as seen in headlines from the early 1930s whirls through our minds: "**PICKETERS HELD IN CONTEMPT,** Holy Year

O.K.'d by Pope, **NAZI SPY GANG IS UNCOVERED**. Bootleg-gers, dope peddlers, and other racketeers, driven into temporary retirement by repeal and other causes, are back of the Boston welfare swindle, it was charged today. . . . Fliers Hop for Rome Tomorrow" (KC, 340). Aiken is so careful to reproduce details of the Cam-bridge-Boston setting that the novel often seems like an urban map, with important landmarks named and located to help place us:

In Massachusetts Avenue the dust whirled under the bright wheels of a streetcar. . . . The Merle was empty, the bookshop was closed. . . . [H]e proceeded toward the post office, along Mount Auburn Street. . . . Ammen zigzagged through the traffic of Tremont Street, was just in time to drop to a walk again at the corner entrance of Houghton and Dutton's. . . . [H]e half turned towards the right, and seemed to be looking fixedly down Court Street. . . . [H]e began to ascend the slight hill to the Court House. . . . [H]e quickened his pace . . . and presently, keeping close to the window of the Waldorf, turned the corner and looked down toward Beacon Street. (KC, 330, 332-34, 338-40)

The streets pass rapidly before us—Reservoir, Huron, Fayer-weather, Gurney, Pemberton Square, Vassal Lane—as do the places: the Beacon Theater, the City Club, Park Street Church, Saint Paul's, Memorial Hall, and the Orpheum. Neighborhood stinks and sights accumulate as we breathe the "sour and acrid smell of slow burning, the animal odor of smoldering human refuse" (KC, 352), and walk with Ammen past "the grotesque shape of the clothes-line in the back yard" (KC, 390-91). If the reader knows the area, he is being placed by Aiken's "facts" on vividly familiar grounds. And even if he has no knowledge of the place, he is being shown a city rendered with such attention to detail that it will convince him of the normalcy of the cityscape.

The more the reader knows of where he is in this novel, the clearer it becomes that Ammen's vision is idiosyncratic. Aiken's strategy for identifying his anti-hero's neurosis works mar-velously, as Ammen uncovers dislocation after dislocation in the "pattern" that he is making for Jones's life. There are simply too many pieces that Ammen can neither foresee nor control nor reduce to a manageable caricature status.

Jasper would like to see Jones as a strangely neutral or abstract emblem of the ultimate monstrosity of life:

> To be sitting here within ten feet of Jones, anonymous embodiment of death, as if they had come together here . . . for the performance of some profound ritual, was . . . the rightest thing in the world. These subhumans, these chattering apes, were the witnesses . . . bore . . . testimony to the perfection and necessity of the idea. . . . Complete in itself, the whole scene had fallen swiftly out of time and space . . . Jones there . . . sniggering . . . the fools clowning under an arranged light . . . the rows of gaping idiots—all this was . . . the awful perfection of the commonplace, the last negation of all values. And if Jones was the negative, he himself was the destructive positive. (KC, 382)

But Ammen discovers that he himself is implicated in Jones's very human suffering, Jones's entanglement in time, with its inevitable—and too often painful and unpredictable—changes. Such doubtful self-assurances as "the stranger had been identified—hadn't he?—as Jones, and as such could thus be destroyed" (KC, 403) will not give Ammen mastery in the face of the painful knowledge of Jones's hopes and poverty, his married life, and the tragedy of his wife's giving birth to a stillborn child. Because Jones is simply a man, like all men, he is subject to forces beyond the control of the human will. Just as Aiken rendered Ammen's obsession in visual terms as a need to reduce the surfaces of his world to controllable patterns, so too it is in visual terms that Aiken convinces us of Ammen's failures. We discover that the man who would reduce other beings to manageable gestures is not even able to manage his own:

> But suddenly he felt he must close his eyes; and opening them again, he as suddenly felt, for no clear reason, that he must clap his hands sharply together before him, turn quickly, look at something else. . . . He . . . walked toward the waterfall without seeing it, revolved quickly away from it, and made as he did so a gesture with his hands such as he knew (and painfully) *he had never in his life made before:* a queer forward thrust of the hands, stiffly parallel, the fingers tensely apart, as if he were in fact *reaching* for something. It lasted only a moment, his arms fell limply to his sides. . . . Once more he began to feel as if he were in some

subtle way being indecently hurried; like a person who in stepping on to an escalator miscalculates its speed. It was as if one were rather cruelly and undignifiedly *yanked,* dislocated—and with that feeling of disgust with oneself which makes one disinclined for the time being to look at oneself in a mirror. To lose *control*— (KC, 403)

With involuntary awkward motions, the puppeteer has become the puppet, the cartoonist his own cartoon.

Jasper Ammen, having expended nearly all of his energy trying to force into existence a visually patterned world, is left by Aiken without the ability to perceive even the simplest physical patterns—clutching at "any fragmentary and lurching vision of a wall or ceiling, to check the wild swoop of his vertigo" (KC, 405). Aiken's final chapter headings make crystal clear just what Ammen's Nietzschean quest to separate himself from, and set himself above, all human relationships has led to: "What It Is To Be a Stranger," "The Stranger Becomes Oneself." Unable to control his environment, unable and unwilling to adapt to it, Ammen is at an impasse. A victim of his inability to exist without separating "self" from other selves and relationships, Ammen's final act (perhaps, really, his *only* action in the novel) is, predictably, one of self-destruction. Conrad Aiken closes the final chapter of this novel with sightlessness, a novel in which the attempt to defeat time with visual images, surfaces, and patterns has been so important: "The gas behind him made a steady sh-h-h-h-h-h-h-. . . . Half past nine. The professor's clock sent its soft *tyang* through the walls. He closed his eyes" (KC, 414).

The completion of his early long prose fictions clearly marks the beginnings of Aiken's widening vision of the human consciousness—of self in relation to its present and to its historical and mythological past and place. Aiken crystallizes themes, techniques, and ideas upon which he was starting to build his verse and upon which he would develop later prose fictions. Speaking in *Ushant* of his grandfather, William James Potter, Aiken provides us with a final perspective on the full breadth of his own achievement to mid-career: "The thing, of course, was not to retreat, never to retreat: never to avoid the full weight of awareness, and all that it brought" (U, 168).

7 At the Circle's Center

"Preludes for Memnon" and "Time in the Rock"

Between June 1928, when he published "Prelude" in *The Dial*, and 9 October 1936, when he published the book *Time in the Rock*, Aiken composed a sustained series of more than 150 meditative lyrics, which together with his poetic exploration of myth and creativity in "Landscape West of Eden" comprise his preludes to attitude and definition ("Preludes for Memnon," 1931; "Landscape West of Eden," 1934; "Time in the Rock," 1936). Perplexing verses, they stand as if at the center of the radiating circles of his life's work, suggesting how clearly assurance "can come, / . . . from the renewed inspection / of a known thing" ("Time in the Rock," SP, 178).

As we have begun to see, Aiken was one of those poets who, discovering a central concern early, found in its gradual uncovering enough energy and variety for continual creative renewal.

> . . . as if the conscious and the unconscious were engaged, had always been engaged, in a dance, the most intricate and surprising and involved and contrapuntal of dances . . . which was one's life: it was against this pressure, and out of it, that his work, his loves, his hatreds and fears . . . had found their—as it now appeared—implicit self-shapings. (U, 242-43)

Aiken was twenty-three when he wrote to T. S. Eliot that "poetry justifies itself, pour moi, only in so far as it is philosophic" (SL, 30). And he was close to seventy-three when he explained in a BBC broadcast to Douglas Bridson that Santayana "most influenced me in the direction of becoming deliberately a philosophic poet" (BBC II, 1)—"providing a greater height from which to see things, and a greater space in which to spread them" (BBC II, 2). Aiken's philosophic preoccupation with the nature of consciousness seemed to be pointing him always toward his goal of obtaining

a simultaneous view of all possible actions and at all possible times. As if the past, the present, and the future, were all presented at once. . . . Could something like this not be the pattern for a work of art? . . . In this sense, therefore, there would be no "progress," or of the ordinary sort, in a work of art: everything past would be hypothecated, everything future would be implied: the movement of these together would constitute a kind of static-dynamic, a stillness of motion round an invisible center. As action would have preceded any given moment in it, so action would follow: but the moment itself, *every* moment, was comprehension. (U, 328-29)

It should not be surprising, then, that after almost two decades of exploring human consciousness from within and from without, turning over the philosophic, psychological, aesthetic and simply artistic-technical implications of the ways one sees and knows a world, Aiken would seek to crystallize the discoveries of his experiments. He created "in those serial essays of his, on attitude and definition . . . *nuclei* of awareness and self-awareness" (U, 320). These were, as Aiken tells it, "a real continued piece of fragmentary soul-searching . . . a sort of combination of idea and feeling and form . . . with the emphasis on the idea" presenting "the analysis of the psyche and the analysis of meaning, or the relationship of language to meaning" (BBC II, 6). He demonstrates what M. L. Rosenthal and Sally M. Gall, writing of the modern poetic sequence, recently described as the "ability to hold in balance conflicting and logically irreconcilable energies . . . felt as mastery over contradiction, mastery by poetic conversion into a pattern of unruly but mobilized affects."[1]

Aiken called this poetry "analytical . . . at bottom . . . in a curious way highly moral. I think the two series of the 'Preludes' are in the nature of precepts. . . . I suppose you could say that the two poems constitute a prolonged fragmentary examination of consciousness, and are also at the same time an approach to a kind of religion without dogma" (BBC II, 7). Yet though created to inform the reader, the verses could not, by the very nature of their message, seek to use the language or form of a poetic essay. In keeping with Aiken's discoveries about the inevitability of change and flow, the interdependent relationships of self and non-self, subject and object, the poems had to avoid systematically separating the parts of the whole experience they were trying to convey. Aiken had to discourse without being simply discursive, to explain but not only referentially. Offering a soliloquy of the mind, the poems' logic nonetheless could not be the language of ideas or science—abstracting, isolating, and ordering some factor as a condition for the comprehension of other ideas or relationships.[2] Trying not to fix the world of change in order to articulate it, Aiken moved, in fact, in these remarkable didactic poems toward the kind of expression that Ernst Cassirer defined as mythic consciousness, a way of apprehending the world in which

consciousness lives in the immediate impression, which it accepts without measuring it by something else. . . . [T]he impression . . . manifests and confirms itself by the simple intensity of its presence, by the irresistible force with which it impresses itself upon consciousness. Whereas scientific thought takes an attitude of inquiry and doubt toward the "object" with its claim to objectivity and necessity, myth knows no such opposition. . . . It has no will to understand the object by encompassing it logically and articulating it with a complex of causes and effects.[3]

Aiken brings together the logical significations of language used discursively with what Hart Crane wrote of as "the so-called illogical impingements of words on the consciousness"[4] that are part of language used expressively. His poems of definition offer a complex gathering of plain speech and what T. E. Hulme once called "an other-world through-the-glass effect"[5]—words used with referential precision and with carefully controlled indirection, contextual regularity, and variation. Thus Aiken presents the essential theme of the importance and danger of man's need to know himself as part of the world in all its interwoven intricacies and variety, all its contraries held in tension:

> There is nothing
> So suits the soul as change.
> . . . .
> You are all things, and all things are your soul.
> ("Preludes for Memnon," SP, 118)

>   surely this
> were nobler answer than the glib speech of habit,
> the well-worn words and ready phrase, that build
> comfortable walls against the wilderness?
> Seeing, to know the terror of seeing: being
> to know the terror of being: knowing, to know
> the dreadfulness of knowledge. . . .
> ("Time in the Rock," SP, 159)

"Preludes for Memnon" and "Time in the Rock"—"the two poems, which really form one poem" (BBC II, 6)—tumbled forth in a flurry of creative activity. Writing to Robert Linscott on 6 December 1930, Aiken exclaimed:

A raging torrent of verse has burst out of me; it can't be stopped; a prelude in the morning is followed by another in the afternoon; all shapes and sizes; all moods and manners. . . . Will you like it? I dunno. But myself, when this morning I went through the whole book of fifty preludes, I was intoxicated. . . . I was fair swep [sic] off my feet. . . . And now in cold blood I take it all back and merely remark that it's a bloody good book, absolutely sui generis, unlike anything ever before, a singular blend of contemporaneous and classic in tone, packed to bursting with ideas, and in a sort of Elizabethan richness of phrasing and rhetoric which wouldn't be too easy to match. That's the kind of swelled head I've got this morning. (WU)

A month later, declaring "a colder and clearer eye than when I last wrote," and still apologizing a bit for fits of "ingrown ego," Aiken wrote of his book-in-the-making as "solidly and emphatically and un-underminably all-of-a-piece" (WU, 15 January 1931).

These are remarkable words for a man rarely given to tooting his own horn, even among friends. The enthusiasm suggests that Aiken, increasingly convinced that "style and form are . . . the explicit manifestations of an implicit mode of thought and feeling" (CC, 63), had found a right way of expressing himself. Aiken's 1962 BBC talk with Douglas Bridson offers a clue to the special, satisfying, formal wholeness of the lyrics:

The fact is that I've always been very much interested in the serial form. . . . And I've used the form in these two poems . . . as possibly the easiest way of getting at the serial nature of Truth. . . . The poem changes constantly—moving by suggestion from one section to another, so that a theme will be taken up and then re-examined in a subsequent section, or re-examined a third time from another point of view. (BBC II, 7)

Exactly what Aiken meant by series is clarified in *Ushant,* where, writing of the serial form of his autobiography with words that clearly reflect upon earlier explorations of serial form as well, Aiken explained:

The series of shapes and symbols—and it was odd to reflect . . . how the idea of "series" had always attracted him—which constituted life, or the language by which one understood life and thus lived it, had . . . become apparently inexhaustible, extending and exfoliating in every direction. (U, 166)

An Aiken series offered, then, moments of meditation and memory that grew, spread out, extended, as if by opening leaves of awareness. Talking later with Bridson, Aiken called this a "sort of spiral," adding yet another leaf to the definition of form that seems, looking back, generally applicable to the "Prelude" series as well as to *Ushant,* which Aiken was discussing at the time.

It's in a way a sort of . . . putting of all the cards on the table, in the way of influences, perceptions and so on. And all in the sort of spiral form . . . going in and out of the memory and to analysis, and back and forth; and without any sort of particular point of entry to begin it with, or any particular point of departure on which to end. But treating experience as a sort of spiral flux which is enterable at any point and departable from at any point. So that the book itself has an annular form if you like. . . . It's like the self-swallowing snake. (BBC II, 4-5)

Realizing the fruitlessness of seeking to "fix" these analytic poems of definition and consciousness—with their "simultaneous view," their fusion of modes, tones, and dictions—yet keeping in mind Aiken's own words in order to clarify ways into the poems, let us turn to the series itself. As the title suggests, many of the poems of "Preludes for Memnon" are lines written as if to be spoken by, or sometimes to provide comment on, Memnon himself, who waits each morning for the world's first light, strangely singing in its arrival. A child of both god and man (son of Eos and Tithonus), slain by Achilles after great battles at Troy, he has become literally a monument to human possibility and limits. As a recent encyclopedic note tells us:

His kingdom was identified with the Egyptian Aethiopia . . . [and] he was connected with the colossal statue of Amenophis near Thebes. This "column of Memnon" is still standing. After its partial destruction by an earthquake in B.C. 27, the musical sound, which it gave forth when touched by the first rays of the sun, was explained as Memnon's greeting to his mother, the Goddess of Dawn. . . . [T]he companions of Memnon, who had been changed into birds . . . on account of their excessive grief for their king came . . . every year to fight and to lament at his grave. The dew-drops of the early morning were called the tears of Eos, which she shed anew every morning in sorrow for her beloved son.[6]

Having passed through the light of life and the darkness of dying, Memnon sings songs that are reflections on the need to understand the nature of transitory human existence and its relation to the wills and worlds of the gods. He greets the light for us all, and his greeting reminds us of change and continuity. His identity is felt in the poem less as a particular being than as a force merging into and out of the worlds of which he sings (or which Aiken sings to him or for him).

The very fact of his voice, raised with the sun each morning, suggests recurrences, the cyclical nature of things in which man must locate himself. Against the realization of cosmic ebb and flow, however, is the awareness of how difficult it is for individuals to order the events that are their lives—and of how strong the instinct toward ordering remains. With language that both organizes and disorganizes the "message," the "Preludes" insist upon the need to accept flux, and yet the poems acknowledge too, both in the questions they raise and the ways they ask them, the inevitable need for patterns. A puzzle raised early in the series is essential:

And how begin, when there is no beginning?
How end, when there's no ending? How cut off
One drop of blood from other, break the stream
. . . .
... Shall we be bold, and say, then, "at this point
The world begins, the windflower ends?" rip out
One bleeding atom, pretend it has no kin? ...
Or shall we, with the powerful mind, hold off
The sky from earth, the earth from sky, to see
Each perish into nothing?
                    ("Preludes for Memnon," SP, 120)

                    They will perish:
The drop of blood, the windflower, and the world;
Sound will be silence; meaning will have no meaning.
The blade of grass, in such a light, will grow
Monstrous as Minotaur; the trick of the clock,—
Should it be taken as the clock's dark secret,—
Is chaos. . . .

. . . .
                    So we pace
. . . .
One chaos and another. Have good heart!
Your chaos is my world; perhaps my chaos
Is world enough for you.
                    ("Preludes for Memnon," SP, 120-21)

"False beginnings will lead you to false endings," as Aiken

states later in "Time in the Rock" (CP, 704). But here Aiken makes certain that we are sure not to begin wrongly. Indeed, we are made to believe there can be no inevitable beginning point, no invariable end; for the world—and the series of words it makes and is made by—is properly perceived as seamless. This lyric is a model of how Aiken manages, in poem after poem, to make his didactic statement and to convince us at the same time that the work is not governed by the piecemeal logic of a linear progression of ideas. From the referential prosiness of the opening query, to the elaborate piling up of figures in apposition to it—explaining and intensifying the query ("blood," "stream," "atom," "windflower"), softening then into the vaguer abstractions of metaphysics ("mind," "time," "nothingness"), returning for a moment to simple referential statement ("So we pace")—the rhythms of expansion and contraction embody in miniature the working of all the "Preludes."

Formulas of communication are collapsing. The poem makes a specific statement about the human condition, and yet we are not sure of even the simplest "facts": Who is the "we"? Where do they "pace," or how? One moment we are observing the smallest units of life as if they are under the lens of some powerful microscope, the next we are gazing out over all the cosmos, as the prelude takes us spiraling through myth, mindscape, philosophy, psychology, the worlds of things and thoughts. Points of attention merge and separate. And our perceptions of wave upon mingling wave of diffusions, implications, and provisos render the "statement" as much as do any of the direct referential lines that the poem contains.

Aiken's rhetorical procedures throughout the "Preludes" compel us out of all complacencies of observation. Poem after poem begins with a conjunction or a preposition. As if starting midline in an interrupted narrative, Aiken fractures the coherence of the unit before us with a sense of its incompleteness as a particular entity; yet he manages simultaneously to suggest its link with a broader continuity and flow just outside our perceptual grasp of the moment: "Or say that in the middle comes a music" ("Preludes for Memnon," CP, 502); "And in the darkness touched a face, and knew" ("Preludes for Memnon," CP, 529); "Or day long watched, in the kaleidoscope" ("Preludes for Memnon," SP, 131).

In the sets of "Preludes," too, versions of a perception are often followed immediately by inversions. The worlds of things and ideas seem constantly, confusedly, turning upside down, inside out, until we are no longer sure if there *is* an up side or a down, an interior or an exterior. Statement is juxtaposed with counterstatement, image with counterimage, in a litany giving us an impression of order in the disorder itself. The rhythmic recurrences, seeming after a time to swell in their gathering, give the weight of religious truth to the mysteries of contradictions. Behind it all, Aiken suggests, looms the shaping power of language.

And there I saw the seed upon the mountain
but it was not a seed it was a star
but it was not a star it was a world
but it was not a world it was a god
but it was not a god it was a laughter. . . .
        ("Time in the Rock," SP, 145-46)

But let us praise the voice the lonely voice
· ·
but let us praise the syllable . . .
. . . which is the seed of worlds. . . .
        ("Time in the Rock," CP, 697)

Of course, as the poet himself is careful to point out, these twists and turns may be regarded simply as semantic trickery.

The world is intricate, and we are nothing.
The world is nothing: we are intricate.
Alas, how simple to invert the world
Inverting phrases!
        ("Preludes for Memnon," SP, 137)

Yet early in "Preludes for Memnon," and increasingly in the lyrics of "Time in the Rock," Aiken makes clear that words and

phrases—and the actions and ideas they convey—self-consciously stated, inverted, and explored from every view, offer our
best ways of glimpsing the truth in all its paradoxical complexity.

>   Add, subtract,
> Divide or subdivide with verbs and adverbs,
> Multiply adjectives like cockatoos
> . . . .
> Or else, with watery parentheses,
> Dilute the current of your pain . . .
> . . . .
> Turn, with a word, the haemorrhage to a glacier;
> And all that . . . we may enjoy (this moment).
> Precisely what we are.
>   ("Preludes for Memnon," SP, 137-38)

"Conceive: be fecundated by the word," Aiken suggests ("Preludes for Memnon," SP, 117). Yet realize too: "Who would carve
words must carve himself / first carve himself" ("Time in the
Rock," SP, 164). Language cannot give us immutability, but the
poet's words can help us grasp the nature of the contradictory,
ever-shifting shapes of the self and of the worlds we both make
and are made by. The poet's gift, and it is no small one, is to "let
us know each single syllable / is ringed with heaven and hell"
("Time in the Rock," CP, 687). His language "sums all, means all,
says all, states the vast end / and vast beginning" ("Time in the
Rock," CP, 687) precisely by calling attention to the limits and
possibilities of coherence, even while making clear the impossibility of fixing the flux of life.

> Surround the thing with words, mark the thing out
> passionately, with all your gestures become words,
> patiently, with all your caution become words,
> your body a single phrase—
>
>   And what do you say—?
> . . . .
> do you tell space or time what the thing is?

Or do you tell the "thing" that it is you!
        ("Time in the Rock," SP, 167)

As we read from prelude to prelude, we hold our attention fast
to obtain our truths of possibility, like Menelaus grasping Pro-
teus as he goes through rapid shifts of shape and being. The
poems present a variety of myths and literary allusions, always
incompletely stated but clearly felt. Among those who come forward to be named are Narcissus and Lesbia, Scylla—"sad child of
time" ("Preludes for Memnon," SP, 119)—"hoar Charybdis"
("Preludes for Memnon," SP, 119), Helen, Clytemnestra, Jesus
and Judas, many winged angels, and of course Memnon—"Stone
feet in sand, stone eyes, stone heart, stone lips, / Who sang the
day before the daybreak came" (SP, 131). Their stories are scat-
tered throughout and are retold in bits and pieces. Their presences offer a sense of continuity, impressions of the breadth and
weight of tradition operating in the series, even as the shadowy
suggestiveness and incompleteness of their presentation adds to
the sense of the flux of things. Aiken is showing us the many faces
of god, who has made man and whom the mind of man has
shaped and reshaped, dreaming of a name for its need for order.
    We are made, too, to apprehend the organic world, alive and in
motion, to recognize the constantly changing designs of which
we are part.

                 Come if you will
to the sea's edge . . .
notice how the wave designs itself . . .
. . . .
froth of a suggestion and then gone.
Notice too the path of the wind in a field of wheat,
the motion indicated.
                ("Time in the Rock" SP, 169)

We move in these series in a stream of words, where past and present, memory, immediate experience and speculation of things to
come all flow together. Each poem is a stepping stone:

At the first stepping-stone, the past of water—
. . . .
. . . the water cold,
. . . the past cold and perfect—

at the second stepping-stone, the present of water,
fluid memory surrounding the cold wish—
. . . .

at the third stepping-stone . . .
suspended poise of the becoming soul—
I was there, I am here, I will be there and gone,
not yet gone, but waiting to be gone—

at the third stepping-stone, the sense of water,
the perfect stream, breakless unchanging all—:
let us wait here . . .
and watch the past and present perpend the future ...
                    ("Time in the Rock," CP, 679)

This is a never completed crossing of the waters of consciousness; we are "never to reach the last, / the final re-
membrance" ("Time in the Rock," CP, 680). But as the poem
makes clear, the journey is essential, not the arrival at some "all-
knowing shore— / where death looks backward from the shad-
ing tree, / and perfect stillness stares at the perfect stream"
("Time in the Rock," CP, 680). We do not reach conclusion, but
we have not travelled pointlessly. For ending here offers not falsi-
fying illusion but rather a sense of having dared to go

To that sheer verge . . .
. . . .
. . . and, looking down,
Search the dark kingdom. It is to self you come,—
And that is God. It is the seed of seeds:
Seed for disastrous and immortal worlds.

It is the answer that no question asked.
                    ("Preludes for Memnon," SP, 123)

We have seen and felt, with Memnon, "In the beginning, chaos, and in the end / Chaos; and the vast wonder come between" ("Preludes for Memnon," CP, 520). We have to come to know that

This is the world: there is no more than this.
The unseen and disastrous prelude, shaking
The trivial act from the terrific action,
Speak: and the ghosts of change, past and to come,
Throng the brief word. The maelstrom has us all.
                    ("Preludes for Memnon," SP, 124)

Along with both the poet and the speaker, refusing easy ordering and the "glib speech of habit, / the well-worn words and ready phrase, that build / comfortable walls against the wilderness" ("Time in the Rock," SP, 159), we experience what it is to "become music, chaos, light, and sound" ("Preludes for Memnon," CP, 518), to say with them for a moment: "I am no longer I: I am a world" ("Preludes for Memnon," CP, 518). As Robert Penn Warren once stated the paradox, in a way that would have appealed immediately to Aiken:

We have lain on the bed and devised evil in the heart.
We have stood in sunlight and named the bad thing good
    and the good thing bad.
. . . .

The recognition of complicity is the beginning of innocence.
The recognition of necessity is the beginning of freedom.
The recognition of the direction of fulfillment is the
    death of the self,
And the death of the self is the beginning of selfhood.
All else is surrogate of hope and destitution of spirit.[7]

Aiken's success in having us comprehend and accept the tensions of contradictory experiences, the imbalances of a disarray of disturbing impressions and ideas, is the result not simply of his ability to compound a short lyric out of a variety of kinds of lan-

guage, symbols, myths. It is the product, too, of the flexible but
definite ordering of the whole of the "Preludes," enabling us to
sense poetic coherence even while accepting a message that
affirms change. Aiken applies a kind of internal image rhyme, an
organic ordering, rather than an architectural one in which units
are built one upon another. He presents generally related but distinct figures that continually thread into and out of each poem
and each other, defining both distinctions and coherences with
their proximities. The result is not a machine made of words but
a biological thing, reminding us to "Keep in the heart"—and
heads—"the journal nature keeps" ("Preludes for Memnon," CP,
547).

The images that surface, entwine, and separate—that generally relate to each other when apart—from beginning to end of
the "Preludes," are those describing nature's plan of growth and
change. From the death of the flower comes seeds that fly and set-
tle to renew life in the roots of the new planting, whose painful
grappling into the earth finally brings forth the plant to continue
the rhythm. The process—and the flowing of water that is part of
it—is clearly associated by Aiken with the contractions and
expansions of the heart sending blood through the body. Clusters
of these images gather and disperse, offering the poem their own
kind of systolic-diastolic rhythms, contraries to each other in the
cycle of things:

And if this heart goes back again to earth,
Taking his anguish with him to make roots,
And his delight for flowers . . .
. . . .
What is there strange. . . .
        ("Preludes for Memnon, CP, 523)

           so it comes from god.
It is the sovereign stream, the source of all;
Bears with it false and true, and dead and dying:
The seed, the seedling: worlds, and worlds to come.
. . . .
Accept this logic, this dark blood of things.
        ("Preludes for Memnon," CP, 536)

I was part of nature's plan;
Knew her cold heart, for I was consciousness;
Came first to hate her, and at last to bless;
Believed in her; doubted; believed again.
My love the lichen had such roots as I,—
The snowflake was my father; I return,
After this interval of faith and question,
To nature's heart, in pain, as I began
      ("Preludes for Memnon, CP, 548)

and there I saw the seed upon the shore
but it was not a seed it was a man
but it was not a man it was a god. . . .
      ("Time in the Rock" SP, 145-46)

There are few poems in our language more difficult than
Aiken's two sets of intentionally didactic "Preludes," mixing as
they do image and idea, symbol and statement into a softly
focused whole whose perpetual motions make it elude direct
grasp. Yet there are few works so satisfying. For if a reader has
been attentive there is no doubt that he will be able to say with the
speaker of "Prelude XLV":

      I have read
Time in the rock and in the human heart,
Space in the bloodstream, and those lesser works
Written by rose and windflower on the summer, sung
By water and snow, deciphered by the eye. . . .
      ("Preludes to Memnon, SP, 135)

8 The Sum
of Worlds
"Landscape West of Eden"

"You are the sum of worlds within and worlds without" (SP, 208), a percipient angel announces to Aiken's poet-personae in "Landscape West of Eden" (1934). The poem is a further clarification of the themes of the "Preludes," and in many ways "Landscape West of Eden" reads like yet another "Prelude" both to attitude and definition—albeit a prelude with a narrative line. But the poem whose making falls between "Preludes for Memnon" and "Time in the Rock" continues to define not only the relation I: World, but also the relations of a poet to his poem and of the poem to the world. Like the series of "Preludes," it is a work about perception. It is also, within the context of Aiken's philosophy of consciousness and change, a poem about poetry—about the poet as maker, the process of making, and the very special, almost religious place of the poet and his work within the flux.

Wallace Stevens, who was the contemporary Aiken most admired, the one he thought "really in a class by himself" (BBC II, 2), offers a view of the poetry-religion-world relation that Aiken no doubt approved:

The relation of art to life is of the first importance especially in a skeptical age since, in the absence of a belief in God, the mind turns to its own creations and examines them, not alone from the aesthetic point of view, but for what they reveal, for what they validate and invalidate, for the support they give.[1]

"God," Stevens wrote, "is a symbol for something that can as well take other forms, as, for example, the form of high poetry."[2] He added, "After one has abandoned a belief in god, poetry is that essence which takes its place as life's redemption."[3] Poetry can redeem a world that often seems defined by incapacity and ugliness. It offers not a system of belief, not even a comfortable harmony, but a flow of perception and emotion that insures the comprehension and, to an extent, the integration of things as they are.[4]

As Aiken noted in a 1931 essay for the *New Freeman* on "The Future of Poetry":

What we want . . . is intensity . . . complete honesty . . . that . . . [the poet] should be religious, without religion. . . . "It is the acme of life"—to quote again from Mr. Santayana—"to understand life. The height of poetry is to speak the language of the gods." ... Or perhaps better—dare I suggest?—to speak the full language of man. (CC,82)

This was the "future" of poetry, perhaps, but for Conrad Aiken it was an inheritance from his grandfather, William James Potter, who lectured "all over the country on the necessity for a religion without dogma" (PR, 120). In fact, Aiken tells us, he regarded himself in many ways as

simply . . . a continuance of my grandfather, and primarily, therefore, . . . a teacher and preacher, and a distributor, in poetic terms, of the *news* of the world, by which I mean new knowledge. . . . I have said repeatedly that as poetry is the highest speech of man, it can not only accept and contain, but in the end express best everything in the world, or in himself, that he discovers. It will absorb and transmute, as it always has done, and glorify, all that we can know. This has always been, and always will be, poetry's office. (PR, 120)

And in the preface that Aiken recreated for "The House of Dust" in 1948, he presented most clearly what "is really, in sum, more or less what . . . Grandfather Potter preached in New Bedford" (PR, 119).

. . . in the evolution of man's consciousness . . . subtilizing his awareness, and in his dedication of himself to this supreme task, man possesses all that he could possibly require in the way of a religious credo: when the half-gods go, the gods arrive; he can, if he only will, become divine. (CP, 1021)

As Aiken told BBC interviewer Douglas Bridson in 1962, when discussing the poems of the "Preludes" period, "I've always rather subscribed to the notion that we are as it were the 'becoming of God'" (BBC II, 8).

I think Hardy somewhat held that view—that we were God's consciousness—I think he went as far as to say that. Or that our consciousness is the coming to consciousness of God. (BBC II, 8)

Implicit in the poems, then, is what Aiken described as a kind of fideism—"something just stopping short of God with a capital G, but nevertheless with a basic faith—and I suppose really a faith in the divinity or the beauty of the Universe,—practically interchangeable terms" (BBC II, 9). Asked by Bridson if that meant that he believed in an evolving universe, Aiken replied: "Yes, I do. I think it's a mobile—to steal Mr. Alexander Calder's term: perpetually changing and recreating itself" (BBC II, 9).

"Angels, but let us have no fantasies," Aiken wrote in "Time in the Rock," elaborating on the nature of his "belief" in the face of a world of elemental flux (SP, 150). "Churches, but let us have no creeds, / no dead gods hung on crosses in a shop, / nor beads nor prayers nor faith nor sin nor penance: / and yet, let us believe, let us believe" (SP, 150).

Let it be the flower
seen by the child for the first time, plucked without thought
broken for love and as soon forgotten:
. . . .

and let the churches be our houses
defiled daily, loud with discord,—
. . . .

let it be self displacing self

as quietly as a child lifts a pebble,
as softly as a flower decides to fall,—
self replacing self
as seed follows flower to earth.
　　("Time in the Rock," SP, 150-51)

What Aiken offers in an age of disbelief is a kind of Santayana-
esque "animal faith," a thing "independent of any revealed or
recorded religion" (BBC II, 9) save as it is realized as exemplifying
one more changing moment among the many. It is a kind of meta-
morphic theology of self, and central amidst the changes is the
poet, orderer and victim of disorder, a being who both is a god of
creation and has his gods.

["Landscape West of Eden"] was one of the ones that was the most fun to
do,—partly because it used a kind of myth-making technique of the
invention of the characters of Adam and Eve and Lilith. . . . The whole
poem resolves itself into a kind of hierarchy of intelligences, going up
from the relative simplicities of Adam and Eve, to the Angel, and then
his angels, and then presumably to other angels still further off. So that
in going backward, forward or up and down this ladder of reference, the
aim is to suggest the total relativity of it all. (BBC II, 10)

The weight of literary associations is unmistakable in the title
"Landscape West of Eden." But upon reading the poem, we find
that we cannot discover either a satisfying schematic clarity of
myth or even a physical specificity in the poem. Neither a naturalistic evocation of the visible world, a portrait through the
senses of an enclosed space, nor a consistent symbolic rendering
of appearances, "Landscape West of Eden" explores a territory of
changing perceptual possibilities. The provocative but deliberately unspecific title yokes together geographical concepts so full
of meaning and confusion as Eden, more than a place, and the
West, as much a promise and a threat as a direction. The immediate suggestion is that we are about to find ourselves in an ambiguous world where intellectual, emotional, and physical considerations are interfused to provide whatever there is in the way
of definitions and impressions of people, places, and ideas.

Even traditional signposts of symbol and geography are some-what unclear. "And the Lord God planted a garden in Eden, in the east" we are told in Genesis 2:8. Before the eastwardness of Eden, though, was the westernness of Elysium, described in Homer's *Odyssey:* "No snow is there, nor yet great storm, nor any rain; but always ocean sendeth forth the breeze of the shrill West to blow cool on men."[5] And Horace directs us to

See, see before us the distant glow
Through the thin dawn-mists of the West
Rich sunlit plains and hilltops gemmed with snow,
The Islands of the Blest![6]

And even after scriptural geography, conceptions of physical and symbolic spiritual place and direction remain complicated—varying from Columbus's certainty of the West as simply a direc-tion travelled to reach, among other places, the East of Eden,[7] to Jonathan Edwards's more complex notions of East and West as more than pointings.

. . . when the Sun of Righteousness, the Sun of the new heavens and new earth comes to rise . . . , the sun shall *rise in the west,* contrary to the course of this world, or the course of things in the old heavens and earth. . . . The Sun of Righteousness has long been going down from east to west; and probably when the time comes of the church's deliv-erance from her enemies . . . the light will rise in the west, until it shines through the world like the sun in its meridian brightness.[8]

For Thoreau, more than a century later, the deadness of the historical past lay eastward; westward was the direction of the apocalypse and of freedom: "Eastward I go only by force; but westward I go free. . . . It is hard for me to believe that I shall find fair landscapes or sufficient wildness and freedom behind the eastern horizon. . . . [B]ut I believe that the forest which I see in the western horizon stretches uninterruptedly toward the setting sun."[9] Yet for so much literature, the West remains the location that reminds us of mortal limits and death. Aiken, rather than selecting from among traditional views, or even adding his own clear synthesis, instead turns his poem on the ambiguities. For as his voice is that of a man who inhabits a world made by forces more potent than himself, his comprehension of space and place is limited; as a godlike creator of his own outer worlds from worlds within, he can take his physical and spiritual bearings only in relation to a self that, at the center of creative energies, is always changing.

From its opening lines, "Landscape West of Eden" seems at once familiar and strange, announcing to the reader both the tradition the poem will work in and divergences. Beginning abruptly, as if in the middle of a narrative we have been following or whose outlines we should know, the poem gradually blurs the reader's comfortable sense of literary regularity. Characters are named whose identity we know ("Eve and Adam, from Eden come with flowerbuds" [SP, 185]) but who seem, in the context of the poem, to be not quite what we expect. Even physical shapes collapse and spaces dissolve. By the end of some fifty lines, though we are not violently dislocated, we are left feeling vaguely discomfited by the ambiguous outline of things.

What seems to be a deliberate grammatical vagueness gives us pause even before the middle of the first line. The language, although not sufficiently obscure to make us stop to wrestle long with meaning, seems only approximately right at best—even when bolstered by a playfully distant reminder of John Milton's syntactic twister: "Of man's first disobedience . . . / Sing."[10] "It was of a deck," we are told—not "on" or "at" one—that we first encounter the speaker and his travelling companions on the mythic journey westward from Eden.

It was of a deck, the prow of a ship, uplifted
by the wide wave of blue and whiteness, swung
. . . by a long wave from the west,
then earthward dropped. And there I, not alone,
westward facing.

        and with me the two children,
Eve and Adam . . .

. . . .
. . . and the long slow sunset
bridled the redfoamed sea, from north across to south,
touching each wavetop with a crimson feather. . . .
                                        (SP, 185)

Before long the semantic confusion of the opening line is somewhat resolved, but then a greater disorientation occurs. We discover the propriety in "of a deck" because it seems for a moment
that the speaker is both *on* and *of* a ship; he is, in fact, the ship
itself, as he describes the action:

                    I lay, rising and falling
as rose the crimsoned waterwaves, remembering
seas, seas, and other seas, and seas before them
above earth, under, and in this kind of dream,—
. . . .
And so I said (but Eve and Adam were silent):
"It is the death and daybreak, all in one;
sow your seeds in the dark, and they will prosper."
                                        (SP, 185)

We realize that the rising and falling of the wavelike motion
marks the breath of the poet in sleep, dreaming his fictive world,
as well as indicates some motion of the voyaging vessel/man
within the frame of the poem. Indeed, levels of verisimilitude
continually give way, one to another, complicating, obscuring,
and clarifying. The "facts," "things," and "objects" of the poem
are not what they seem. For the poem is not essentially mimetic
but is rather a phenomenological encounter with the "facts" of the
maker's mind at work, compelling us to perceive the nature of
creating. The poet and his poetic objects share an identity; the
maker of fictions sets life in motion, remains apart from it, yet
participates in it as well.

"Not being God" (SP, 186), the speaker tells us, if he cannot
"persuade" his characters to do his bidding, he would not "wish /
to alter the inalterable" (SP, 186). Yet clearly he is, for his work,
what he allows himself to be called: "Mortal god" (SP, 203),

"infant god" (SP, 204), and for the Adam and Eve of his making,
"our god" (SP, 205). A god of creation as well as a limited being
subject to other incomprehensible creative energies, he makes
worlds in his mind's eye that satisfy by clarifying hitherto unor-
dered ideas and feelings, yet that terrify with unknown places,
hidden even to the self that made them. There are places westward:

And this dream-ship dissolved into evening light
. . . .
and the one island left that was myself—
this sunset-thought, here at the western window . . .
. . . .
. . . now my thoughts
bring back those images of Eve and Adam
to me once more, who sent them forth; and the angel too
who was myself come home.

. . . .
. . . forthgoing from the window in my thought's power,
I climb the hill in sunset light, going westward;
. . . .

          Remembering the "out there" and the
               "here within,"
this little coral island of the mind,
broken upon with all the foams of nescience. . . .
                                        (SP, 187-88)

And later there are explorations eastward:

Thus from the window eastward faring in thought I went,
. . . .
. . . spreading imagination's widening wings;
and saw the origin, . . .
. . . .
And must we know—I thought sadly—the unknown?
why must we seek it?
                                        (SP, 204)

In the poem's "desperate voyages to . . . unknown coasts" (SP,
186)—going west toward knowledge of endings, the promise of
the future, and the certainty of dying, and heading east seeking
beginnings, "the void of the unknowable, whence we come" (SP,
204)—man and woman and man-god echo in each other the tensions and confusions implicit in the "splendid thirst for knowledge" (SP, 207), the struggle to break boundaries. Adam and Eve,
finally looking eastward too, quarrel with each other and with
their maker-god who is pleased, pitying, and "angry / . . . they
should mimic . . . unwitting, / the agonies of gods" in seeking
comprehension beyond their limits (SP, 206-7). And the poet-
creator himself wrestles with *his* "satirical angel" (SP, 191), the
"dark angel" (SP, 199) who in fact speaks as an "angel-self" (SP,
190), a sort of alter ego whose temptations add a new direction,
southward, which must be understood if the poet's journey
toward the truths of human nature and the potentials of artistic
creation are not to be misconstrued as simply prideful madness
or stubborn stupidity. For while this "minstrel fellow whom [the
poet] hated" (SP, 186) can be readily denigrated as a "dilapidated
angel-self, with ragged wings" (SP, 190), "no larger than a mos-
quito above the trees" (SP, 194), his seductive song of "flight /
southward" to "heart-warmth" (SP, 204), ease, and avoidance is
nonetheless strong and persistent. It is an inevitable and important mind-made part of the agony in the pursuit of "the countless
planes of feeling, or of knowledge, or of guess, / of which a
moment's awareness is the intersection" (SP, 207). One must
know what one runs from as well as looks toward. There are risks
both behind and before the seeker once he has taken a first step
beyond simple acceptance of habitual truths: "the tragedy of the
half-remembered, the half-longed for; / perceptions of time, of
distance; self distrust, self praise / . . . / . . . the new decision /
made in the nerve-cell!" (SP, 207-8).

Finally, though, even worldly southwardness must be
embraced as part of human possibility and recognized for the violently impassioned place it is, not shunned simply as a dangerous
temptation to inaction when pursuing nobler directions. Thus
the speaker's final angelic creature, Lilith, springs from his pre-

conscious to represent the southern, sensual region not as a voice
of shrewd logic, offering relief as one wanders toward dangerous
frontiers of knowing, but as the more immediate presence of
intensely felt sensual passions, the underside of familiar things, a
different kind of knowing.

It was when Lilith became an angel that I learned
. . . how language too
leads one perforce into the south of worldmake.
. . . .
hiding her face she laughed a little, and spoke

. . . .
"Come, god, and see how evil can flower in purple!
Come with me, I will teach you how the kiss
creates such kingdoms as your pure Adam never dreamed."

Strange, too, the imaginations that she gave me
out of her voice and eyes, while, daylong and nightlong,
under the farthest nothing, we hung embraced.
. . . .
already half distinct I saw that fevered world;
inchoate lewdness becoming shapes,
shadows becoming lurid delicious lights,
all whirling, mad, and with delirium's wonder,
splendours of foulness. I withdrew my lips
from Lilith's lips, beat my right wing, and turned
to stare more soberly at this world of evil.

                                    (SP, 208-9)

It is a world that must be felt and seen. For the experience of
darkness, along with the other explorations of the brighter places
of sunrise and sunset, offers knowledge of this world in all its perplexing motion. These, together with a realization of the mind's
longing for release from change, for languor and numbness, dem-
onstrate throughout the poem "how false this world, how true,
and what its power" (SP, 209).

    What Aiken has managed in this exploration of poetic pos-
sibility is well summed in one of his poet-god speaker's most
striking pronouncements:

It was myself I thus dispersed,
thus with a thought altered to new pattern
for the delight in change, and the delight in knowing
the old order now forever fixed and inalterable;
fixed in memory, but changed by thought of change;
for nothing changes but thinking makes it change.

                              (SP, 191-92)

"Thus," we are told—and we cannot help agreeing, we who have journeyed with Aiken through worlds both known and unknown—"I renewed / the world within, the world without, world without end" (SP, 192).

9 The Country Clock Wound Up Again
Rediscovering America

The question "what next?" is no small one for a poet who has published a Pulitzer Prize-winning volume of *Selected Poems* (1929) and has just completed major works that are summings-up of more than twenty-five years of productive writing. Aiken's series of beautiful love sonnets, "And in the Human Heart," many of which he included in letters to his wife Mary during seven weeks of separation in 1939, are so closely linked to his earlier studies of human consciousness as to derive their title from the same lines in "Preludes for Memnon" that provided the title for "Time in the Rock": "I have read / Time in the rock and in the human heart" (SP, 135). And as Jay Martin aptly explains of another work of the period, "Blues for Ruby Matrix":

Although it was not published until 1942, in the *Brownstone Eclogues* volume, "Ruby Matrix" is contemporaneous with the Preludes. Like them it arises from Aiken's discovery of the . . . resemblance between "the word, the world, the wound" (T.R., VIII, 672)—between the individual and his universe and the language through which he can understand and express this relationship.[1]

Brownstone Eclogues continued to explore the soul of the city encountered earlier in "Turns and Movies," "The House of Dust" and "Senlin," whereas "The Soldier" (1944) offered one more page in Aiken's ongoing book of changing consciousness. As Aiken wrote to Malcolm Cowley in 1946, somewhat acidly evaluating his own career:

Here you can see a young man who fondly thought he was seeking a kind of absolute music in word and verse, when in reality he was embarking, unknown to himself, on a psychoanalytic celebration of the con-sciousness of modern man, a celebration which took the form of five overlapping symphonies; Changing Mind; Landscape West of Eden; The Soldier, and two volumes of so-called preludes; not to mention sun-dry other false starts, dead ends, and intercalary experiments. (SL, 268)

These are fine poems, as rich and resonant as many in Aiken's career. But coming after "Landscape West of Eden" and the two sets of "Preludes," they read more often than not like after-thoughts to his major achievements. Still, for Aiken these years just before, during, and after World War II *were* years of creative renewal. Rediscovery and growth did not occur at once; nor did it result in works that were either completely successful or com-pletely new. Fresh poetic impulses coexisted with old. Works on established themes continued to be written in established ways even as new themes and formulations were conceived. And, of course, new themes drew on old, blending with them, transform-ing or transmuting them.

What happened to Aiken was that he rediscovered America, finding in the second half of the 1930s that his "country clock was wound up again" (U, 337)—wound, in fact, in a way it had never been before. Always moved by "a secret dualism that profoundly suited him" (U, 134)—swinging between the stability of forms in England, the old country, and the vitality and freedom in Amer-ica, the new—Aiken now found himself vigorously drawn to "so much in America that was still virginal and tentative" (U, 134). Partly because of the beginning of the Second World War, which compelled departure from Europe where he had most recently been living, partly because of the dissolution of one marriage fol-lowed by the pleasures of another, and partly because of the emp-tiness that ineluctably followed a culmination to a part of his writing career, Aiken was ripe for change. He was ready to seize the opportunity to encounter the "new civilization, the new culture . . . still in the process of formation, of evolution" (U, 137). The "shadow of the Old Country," which for years had been "falling with a disturbing and revealing suggestiveness on the simple planes of the new" (U, 135), lifted. Aiken, after submitting to the delicious intoxications of the old world—"perhaps to the point of becoming himself a saturated solution" (U, 135)—could "enjoy the American scene whole heartedly again" (U, 135).

His enjoyment now, however, was not at the expense of attractions of the old world, but was in reconciliation with them. The near schizophrenia of the English-American love-hate that had been a factor in Aiken's life for years is amply documented. Consider, for example, the contrasting notes to Robert Linscott in 1921 and to Theodore Spencer in 1930:

Dear Bob: . . . Here we are—utterly miserable, fog-enclosed, sunless, cold. . . . [T]he English stagger me, paralyze me. . . . Have the English any feelings—or do they hide them on the theory that they are things which no civilized person would confess to? . . . England would be so nice if it was inhabited by Americans! (SL, 62-63)

. . . SIR I resent the suggestion that I am a maggot in a dead lion. . . . Pour moi, America is a weariness of the flesh and spirit; I do no work there. . . . Here, I actually feel like working, and actually have begun to work. . . . Not that I don't like America. . . . I could cheerfully have stayed there forever, but a pricking conscience said why not go to England, where you'll die of melancholy and nostalgia and do some work before you die, bad or good? A little enforced misery to heaven knows what end.—And on the whole I think this is a better life. Serener. Simpler. More real. . . . Perhaps even, when one thinks of the landscape and the speech and the tempo, more beautiful. (SL, 160-61)

At last, having lived, worked, and fruitfully created amidst the trappings of old world and new, and having discovered intermittently his ties with both, Aiken was able to find in ancestral voices a way to comprehend the inseparable intertwining of his old and new country roots—the traditions of the past, the intense sense of the present, the promise of the future and change. As he tells it in *Ushant,* "Ultimately, there needed to be no semantic gulf, no Atlantic, between Savannah (or New Bedford) and London" (U, 138).

Of course, the subject of American voices and places had long been one of Aiken's imaginative resources. He once told an interviewer "I have never thought of myself as a *New Englander*—I think of myself as a *writer*. But I went to the Middlesex School, in Concord, and naturally the Emerson-Thoreau-Hawthorne thing went into my gizzard" (Shenandoah, 22). Yet he did not directly explore much of his American inheritance and the themes of American place, myth, and personality until his 1937 essay "Literature," written as part of the Federal Writers' WPA compilation *Massachusetts: A Guide to Its Places and People*. While doing research for the piece, he tells us, he rediscovered William Blackstone, first settler of Boston, the "prototypically" (U, 288) American figure who had been at the back of Aiken's mind for some twenty years.[2] For the poet newly returned to America, this scholar-explorer—"this young Cambridge graduate with his books . . . his conscience, and his passionate desire for privacy," his "perpetual centrifugal retreat from civilization, whenever it managed to catch up with him" (CC, 83)—seemed "a magical figure" (U, 288) of stability and stimulation. Blackstone was Aiken's catalyst to a new phase of imaginative growth, was the

"open sesame" not only to a truer understanding of the American scene and character than any hitherto available, in its rare combination of purity and singleness of purpose, its entire naturalness, and the complete unself-consciousness of its love, but also . . . a revelation of something unsuspected in himself. Those apple-trees, tenderly set out by the young divine from England, on the three-pointed hill purchased from the Shawmut Indians . . . those apple-trees had roots, somehow, he began anew to feel, in himself. . . . And couldn't one . . . take him as the spiritual key, or center, of a book on American individualism? Wasn't he the complete and unmistakable forerunner? . . . [W]eren't they all to be in this sense frontiersmen, pioneers, solitaries, outlaws? those who preferred to seek, and find, alone? (U, 289-90)

The specific project for which "the notes had been made, the reading outlined, even a preliminary paragraph or two . . . set down" (U, 290) was not completed until the spring of 1947, when the Blackstone poem, "The Kid," was first published in *Western Review*.[3] In the intervening years, Aiken began to explore his newly discovered territory, first somewhat tentatively and with mixed results in his last two novels, *A Heart for the Gods of Mexico* and *Conversation,* and then more directly in new poems like "Mayflower," which merged his specific American themes and their complicated relationship to his interest in European forms into his more general, lifelong exploration of human consciousness.

10 Live for the Borderland
A Heart for the Gods of Mexico and Conversation

On 15 February 1935, months before the publication of his third novel, *King Coffin,* Aiken wrote to his friend Robert Linscott of his financial worries, and his mental weariness:

I feel full of odds and ends of notions and curiosities, more than for years, and would like to take a longish period of . . . gestation to sort them out into something really good . . . this week-to-week sort of life with bills hanging over us and the future always so dark isn't conducive to settled and *serene* work, and it's the serene thing I want to get at now—my hectic days are over, *Great Circle* I think marked an end to that phase, I don't expect any more explosions. (WU)

But "explosions" continued, impelled by the restlessness of Aiken's imagination, by the necessities of nonstop publishing in order to resolve financial difficulties,[1] and finally by the rediscovery of his homeland. His new works expressed the tensions of his contradictory longings: on the one hand for stable, old country domestic worlds of contented repose, defined by known, bounded spaces, fixed forms, measured and measurable activities, and on the other hand for adventurous new worlds in which he could explore his own consciousness, bringing both a self and a world into being while passing through unknown territories.

Of course, the themes were not new ones; nor were they strictly personal ones. In fact, if American fiction can be said to have a tradition, it is one defined precisely by the tensions involved in the impulses to create domestic fictions and new

124

world fictions: to render narratives that regard social forms as more important than imaginative explorations of unbounded spaces (an inherited European tradition) and to render narratives that are spun out of traditions of new world exploration tales and travel books, asserting the importance of exploration of the frontiers of land and mind.[2]

Yet Aiken, in addition to being an exemplar and inheritor of an American tradition, was a developer of one as well. What makes Aiken's last two novels—*A Heart for the Gods of Mexico* (1939) and *Conversation* (1940)—so remarkable is not only that they present a dualism of domesticity and adventurous freedom that is somehow both elementally American and highly personal, but also that his characters are intensely aware of the dualism, without having to deny or negate the paradoxes that they cannot solve. These works, far from being primarily explorations of a private self, as were Aiken's earlier novels, explicitly focus on their characters' relation to place: to home and community, to the land, to the myths and metaphors that are part of a distinctly American experience, and to the history of American settlement. The idea of America becomes a main "character," affecting individual lives, yet containing a life of its own. The two novels are especially enlightening in the ways their developing American concerns help crystallize for the reader Aiken's main ideas and achievements as a novelist whose fictions represent a reality in which men both define and are defined by the worlds they inhabit.

The publication history of Aiken's ambitious, though admittedly flawed, last novels is a sad one. By the time *Ushant* was published in 1952, Aiken had joined the vox populi in concluding the works to be failures. Perhaps he overreacted to criticism; certainly he was viewing the works from a more secure vantage, having by that time demonstrated his ability to control the creative energies released in the late 1930s with the rediscovery of American themes. His evaluation of *A Heart for the Gods of Mexico* was especially astringent, as he commented on

that melancholy and half-finished project, *A Heart for the Barranca* [*A*

Heart for the Gods of Mexico]. . . . Six months later. . . and no doubt as a result of this very piece of desperate unsuccess, he had found himself, for *The Quarrel* [*Conversation*], in a complete state of readiness. One could complain of it that it was slight, certainly, but compared with *A Heart for the Barranca* it was at least alive. . . . Thanks to the *Barranca,* the machine was working again. . . . Of course he had been too close to it: he had tried to rush it. (U, 342)

Yet although *A Heart for the Gods of Mexico* is strangely foreshortened, as if brought to a halt by its author's lack of time, energy, and patience in his need to get something in print, and though *Conversation* seems sometimes static and has a conclusion that seems too neat, both novels were cleverly conceived, often written with great beauty and insight, and Aiken believed in both at their inceptions. His faith was put to an early test.

"Novelette ²/₃ done: viz, about 22000" (WU), he wrote to Robert Linscott on 3 December 1937 about what was to become *A Heart for the Gods of Mexico.* Nine months later, on 2 September 1938, he wrote: "Secker has taken my novelette here—but the situation in the U S seems dark. Bernice muttered something about the Countryman Press doing a limited edition, not so good, and I countered with objections, so I don't know what happens. A sad end to a whole winter's work—not a sou from America, and only $100 from Secker. What's the use. And everybody likes the thing, too, and I'm myself persuaded it could be made to sell" (WU).³ Only four months more and Aiken was defending the work, which had still failed to generate interest in his homeland.

Linsk. . . I am saddened by your indifference to Mexico, which myself I think good, say what you will . . . and classical in form—this is one of the days when I feel confident about it, after many, many more, when I viewed it with a somber blue lacklustre stale-oyster eye—so forgive me if in defense I lay on the self-praise with a golden trowel. Not that I think it great, or profound, or vast, or anything like that—but it's a genuine poem for all that, and so much better than 99% of the labored trash that passes as fiction that I will wager you a purple bible against a decayed molar that ten years from now it will be ensconced in a nice little glass-lined niche of its own, when all the best sellers and books of the month and pseudo-literary works of this day are long since pulped. . . . Any takers? No, you won't play, and I know it, blast you, so send me back my little book, will you please, as quick as you can, so that if I get a brain wave about somewhere else to try it on I can do so. . . . [I]t comes out here next month, and I can at least nourish a somewhat ailing hope that it will struggle to such minor success in London that it may then swim its way across the sea to *your* inhospitable shores. (WU, 31 December 1938)

Conversation (1940) was an equal agony: "When I consider Great Circle, King Coffin, and Mexico, all flopping one after another, I despair. The new one is called The Conversation: or, Pilgrim's Progress, and is a sinfonia domestica. . . . I have a feeling that it's terribly alive, people, background everything—that's when I have a moment of confidence. But I also have a dread that it may be very dull. . . . Anyway, it's done" (WU, 20 May 1939). The reading public was demonstrating once again what Aiken had stated before—perhaps optimistically, perhaps ironically, perhaps desperately: "We isolate, we exile our great men, whether by ignoring them or praising them stupidly. And perhaps this isolation we offer them is our greatest gift" (CC, 49).

The earlier of Aiken's unappreciated novels of American rediscovery, *A Heart for the Gods of Mexico*—based loosely on the experience of a trip taken to Mexico by Aiken, Mary Hoover, who was soon to be his wife, and a friend, the British painter Edward Burra—records the journey of three central characters from home in Boston to the unknown in Cuernavaca. It is a tale of interpenetrating lives and frontier explorations, which challenges throughout the notion of the antithesis between what we will call here "domesticity" (comfortable, established forms) and wilderness adventure (the American frontier experience updated). We discover that domesticity without the promise of openness and new experience is stultifying at best, corrupting at worst, and in its rigidity of forms, paradoxically offers much the same sort of insecurity that one might expect in the instabilities of the adventurous experience. And the openness of wilderness adventures seems always to involve in part the human impulse toward shaping the unshaped. For good or for ill the domestic and wilderness experiences entwine. The shifting rhythms of the novel continually merge and reverse concepts of civilized and primitive, formal and unformed, objective and subjective, in order to show us that each condition seems to contain the seeds, if not the flowers, of its alternative. Aiken insures that we will remember, as Wallace Stevens puts it in "Connoisseur of Chaos":

A. A violent order is disorder; and
B. A great disorder is an order. These
Two things are one.[4]

Noni, Blom, and Gil, the novel's three protagonists, depart from a world where fixed social forms have become so ritualized as to be suffocating, and they move toward what promises to be an enchanted world ˌwhere time is transformed into both a mythic past and, paradoxically, a complete present. Here social norms, it would seem, are submerged into original chaos. It is a journey toward death literally for one of the three (Noni is dying of heart disease) and figuratively—toward a death of the old ways—for one of the other two. It promises, too, a death into life, a dissolution of one kind of existence and the simultaneous rebirth of the individual self, marked by participation in the process of experience as the trip progresses. And yet Aiken makes clear that this journey by train across the heartland of America and into unknown spaces does not so much leave behind old worlds as transubstantiate them. Amidst the known rituals of social life, the trip offers one last behavioral ritual of death, whose enactment, rather than shucking off the old world of domestic forms, rediscovers and affirms, in these forms, the possibilities of discovery and adventure. The basic values of the group, now comprehended through the needs of the individual explorer, emerge strengthened by the trip into chaos, the journey of civilization into its own origins.

A Heart for the Gods of Mexico is a novel in motion from its opening page to its last. We are moved first on foot and subway through the city of Boston and its environs, then by train through upper New York state and the midwestern plains of the United States, and finally by car over dark and dangerous Mexican mountains into the storm-ridden town of Cuernavaca. Yet the novel's opening is remarkably static. Scenes seem particularized and frozen. Boston assembles itself for us in reduplicating pieces, with each place, each scene, seeming to vary very slightly, if at all, from the last. The effect is similar to that of seeing a group of still photos of familiar places laid side by side.

First impressions are, of course, very important in any fictive encounter, providing us with the frame of reference against which we can measure our sense of dramatic development. And first impressions in *A Heart for the Gods of Mexico* are almost stiflingly comfortable and familiar, despite the great potential for discomforting dramatic tension in the events surrounding a moment of crisis in the affairs of Blomberg and his soon-to-be-married friends, Noni (who is dying) and Gil (who does not know it). The stakes seem to be uncommonly high as Blom solicits wedding-trip money from a wealthy friend, ironically and aptly named "Key." Yet we are not made to doubt the outcome of the encounter. Blom will surely get his money, and he and his friends will just as surely make the trip to Mexico. Our attention is directed not toward the action at hand, but toward the way the episode is handled by the two men involved. In the world of the novel's opening we are invited to notice not events, but habitual behavioral patterns. The discrepancy, though, between the tension implied by the event and the commonness of its enactment turns the comfort into discomfort even as we experience the old familiar places and people. Social codes prevail in Boston's domestic scene, but the plot promises apocalyptic moments, self-discoveries, marriage, death. Because of the circumstances of Noni's fatal illness and the planned escape to Mexico, the reader does not yet expect only, or even primarily, the usual. The known world of the city, then, governed by unshakable and ever-predictable behavioral patterns, is both comforting and threatening in its obliviousness to the fragile and changeable human condition. Too, details are made to persistently impinge meanings on our unconscious, hinting vaguely that unease exists near the level of appearances. The effect of the opening chapter is, finally, what Blom half jokingly calls in the very first sentence of the novel "ommernous" (HFG, 417).

Blom and Key meet near the Frog Pond in Boston Common, and we follow their winding way through the city as if walking behind them with a camera and a microphone, recording the surface details of their encounter. We perceive an environment without inwardness or depth, a world of organized sounds, geometric patterns, and mirrored reflections that, it seems, the eye and ear can readily control. Yet the details are unsettling and troublesome as well, implying that even at the surface, below which we are not permitted to see, things are not *quite* right. With Blom, who "avoid[s] looking at his reflection in the glassy water," we play a kind of game, walking "as close as possible to the pond's edge, along the familiar granite curbing . . . enjoy[ing] the notion of his image . . . stalking angularly among budding boughs against a twilight May sky" (HFG, 417). We move in a linear world of cartoons—"there before him was Key coming . . . cockily on his short legs, the derby hat set crookedly like a tiny peanut on the tiny head, the dark glasses looking blind above the already smiling mouth" (HFG, 417). Yet we also pass pictorially naturalistic street scenes whose details are attentively rendered but that even here disturb us with their impressionistic suggestions of more than commonplace occurrences:

They veered . . . towards the gravel expanse of the baseball field in the Boylston Street corner of the Common, now beginning to look gray in the vanishing light of evening. The sweet sound of a batted ball, tingling and round and willowy, floated up to them, and they turned their eyes towards the gray-flanneled figures which moved there in the dusk. . . . [O]ne of the players . . . small white face lifted to the sky, performed [a] crablike balance dance under the heaven-descending ball, until the sharply lowered elbows, and barely heard *clop,* showed that it had been caught. Beyond the field, lights were beginning to come out in the Boylston Street Shops. (HFG, 418)

There is pleasure in the wandering eye's casual perception of domestic scenes of things-as-the-are and things generally as they ought-to-be, of a multiplicity of life that can be appreciated without the necessity of any commitment to an intensely felt experience. But the description, too, is like a part of some ritual enactment whose import we cannot grasp, but which suggests that amidst the objectively comforting and familiar scene something is askew, either with the perceiver or the thing perceived.

We slow with Blom and Key to observe "the gay windows of the Nip, with its hospitably open door" (HFG, 419). With a feeling that everything is "amusingly in character" (HFG, 420), we eavesdrop on what seems to be a conversational game of wits as Blom angles for the right moment to ask for help and Key holds him off awhile for the pleasure of the sport. There is chatter over drinks and oblique discussion of Noni and Gil over "lamb with okra" (HFG, 421). Only sporadically, while we observe the pleasant formalities of eating, does Aiken allow his characters to discuss directly and openly the reasons for their having come together on this evening. While the two "[eat] their oysters in silence . . . still for a moment, as for the completion of a ritual" (HFG, 421), the reader's frustration grows. The very sense of evenness and balance becomes unsettling in its sterile sameness and featurelessness: "In a front booth, from which they looked out at the . . . lamplit rear walls—smooth and sinister as precipices—of the Metropolitan Theater—a view which unaccountably always made Blomberg think of Hamlet and Elsinore—they studied the pale blue mimeograph of the menu" (HFG, 421). And the tragic implications of Noni's coming death, together with the idea of a rebirth of wonder if only for a short time in Mexico, make us feel strongly how awful is the indifferent changeless face of things.

The stilted motions of chapter one provide a touchstone for measuring the far more extreme movements of chapters two and three, where we enter a transitional world someplace between the domestic regularity of Boston and the longed-for transforming environment of a Mexican land of enchantment. With Noni introduced as our spiritual guide, seeming to embody the very notion of change—"as a matter of fact you don't know quite *what* she looks like, somehow, because what you always notice in her face is the movement, the light"(HFG, 426)—the first chapter ends by inviting the reader to contemplate the excitement, the promise, the risk, and the terror of pushing off into what seems to be unknown and therefore undefined (perhaps undefinable) space.

This time tomorrow, where in God's name would they be? In a strange world, on their way to the unknown. . . . Mexico, that fabulous land, that land of savage ghosts and bloodstained altars, began to swirl. . . . "We'll be like babes in the wood—none of us ever went west of the Hudson before." . . . He smiled grimly, and whistled a ghost of a Bach tune . . . and once more the sound and swiftness of the journey came around him, palpable almost as a stream of light or water. The wheels, the bells, the whistles, the sliding and whirling land, the centripetal and tumultuous descent into the Inferno, the descent into Mexico. (HFG, 429-33)

Having already been introduced to an idea of the individual identity that seems to be clearly linked to life experienced through continuities, recurrences, and habits, we suddenly discover a situation in which people and places seem for a moment to be dislocated in space and time. The gaze, accustomed to turning outward to see only what it expects to see, is compelled outward and inward simultaneously: outward to see clearly for the first time scenes for which it has no simple formulaic frame of reference; inward to discover the psychic conditions that will stamp the perception of these unknown places, as the eye half perceives and half creates its world. In scenes strikingly reminiscent of "The River" section of Hart Crane's *The Bridge*, we look from the protected vantage of one of civilization's most significant modern creations, the train, at an American landscape in its uncorrupted form. As discontinuities assemble, the sense of looking at the world from a safe arena—from the viewpoint of a little bit of civilization carried into the wilderness—diminishes. And all the while Aiken's descriptive language works to reinforce the growing sense of confusion and dislocation. Although the faint echo of a "Bach tune" may tick off its contrapuntal precisions in Blom's mind, the reader is engulfed by the swelling cacophony of often undifferentiated sounds.

Before long, though, the rhythm of the wheels becomes repetitive, recognizable, even predictable in its regularity, sounding out familiar places—*"Boston and Albany—Boston and Albany—Boston and Albany—Boston—Springfield—Westfield—Pittsfield"* (HFG, 433)—as if to remind us ironically that this is, after all, simply a well-travelled route. But the train keeps moving toward the unknown, seeming to carry Noni, Gil, Blom, and the reader inexorably out into a void: "Everything had dissolved in time and sound . . . the only remaining reality was the train. The earth was a dream, the past was a dream" (HFG, 433). Here, where the travellers have lost their familiar houses, streets, and persons, there seems initially no sense of history. Aiken's characters learn just how important for self-definition was their sense of being participants in the life of a specific place.

Boston was gone, and the Berkshire hills . . . had fled soundlessly away into a past which had now neither meaning nor existence. Those people might still be there, the Berkshires might still be there . . . but the train, hollowing a golden and evanescent tunnel through the darkness, fleeting and impermanent as a falling star, denied all things but itself. (HFG, 433)

Yet feelings of hollowness and loss, which accompany the dissolution of a world of identity-sustaining external forms, quickly give way to suggestions of the exhilaration of recognizing, with Blom as our discoverer, that a sense of identity can come from within as well as from without. An internal sense of place can offer one a sense of historical moment and can help one comprehend the external place itself, as well as the other way round. In fact, the realities of presumably subjective inner worlds and seemingly objective outer worlds may be inseparable.

And so on to the train and into motion, and out of time, too, in the sense that they had now *become* time. All day, all night, the landscape whirling and unfolding and again folding, rising and falling, swooping and melting, opening and shutting. Blomberg gliding evenly among the haunted birches and junipers of the Berkshires, a puritan among the puritans. . . . Blomberg defending the stockade at Deerfield in deep snow, Blomberg bowling at ninepins with the Dutch trolls of the Catskills, Blomberg gazing down from the railway bridge at Hendrik Hudson's little ship. (HFG, 434)

The ride is "unreal" (HFG, 434), because up until now only what we already know has given shape to our reality. But the trip is "also [becoming] uncannily real" (HFG, 434), taking us all "to the west, the south . . . [and] into the darkness" (HFG, 434) where our essential selves exist. It is a dangerous ride into "nothing" (HFG, 434) known; yet it seems to plunge us into the waters of our inner beings—the "soul's dwelling place" (HFG, 438), "marvellously pure and clear, and . . . deep" (HFG, 438). It is an experience like looking into "the very center of the earth" (HFG, 438), an experience of the "real, the business of settling into the empty car . . . while they climbed swiftly, and then less swiftly . . . settling into this motion, this principle of placelessness" (HFG, 434).

> Noni . . . knew the night, in its half-sleep her whole body was aware of the violent magic of time and place which was affronting them. . . . With her eyes closed, she was *living* time, feeling it and taking it, this minute and the next and the next, this hour, this transit, this speed, and all the complication of texture with which they were woven. (HFG, 435)

Still, the very experience of displacement in travelling has done more than necessitate self-definition. It has thrown two of Aiken's three protagonists together in a way that has enabled them to understand each other better. As the trip makes us aware of the development of individual consciousness, so too it makes us aware that external relationships, the very cornerstones of domesticity, can be even more important in a world without fixed forms to adhere to and rigid roles to play. Gil, of course, is not informed of Noni's illness and so has not radically risked the old domestic world. He remains protected from such loss, and its ensuing breakdown of familiar patterns, by his travelling companions' conspiracy of silence. His trip in fact is a kind of extension of domestic forms, as it is to end in marriage, the most important domestic ritual of all. Blom and Noni, however, are together separated from familiar things by the fact of death as well as by distance. They are compelled, without the distracting demands of fitting their behavior toward one another into an external code, to experience their relationship more honestly. Facing together an unknown world, they can begin to understand both the new and the old worlds better; they can see more clearly the nature of the closeness that was so essential a part of the old pattern.

They exchanged a leisurely look of unhurried understanding, in which all the future lay between them like a long-familiar landscape, every beloved feature of which was wonderfully known to them . . . the years like seed, the years like furrows, the years like sheaves. Noni at Nonquitt, freckled, sailing an eighteen-footer; Noni in Boston, bringing back a basket of daffodils and music from Faneuil Hall. . . . Noni with himself and her devoted Gil, and then—Gil and himself alone, looking back. . . . And as they gazed at each other . . . it was as if, in the wide landscape of all life, they could see themselves . . . always where ever they happened to be going, with perfect knowledge of a shared purpose and view, a known and accepted destiny. This was their life. This had been their life. (HFG, 460)

At the midpoint of the turning world lies St. Louis, end of all points east, gateway to the West. The city's shabbiness reminds us one last time of how destructive society's domesticating patterns can be, offering vacancies and instabilities rather than formal solidities. Even the language, so orderly in contrast to the verbal turbulence of the descriptions of the train ride, seems leaden—little more than an empty list of descriptive items. The whole shell of what once was or might have been is "meretricious, . . . streets that were spacious, but without beauty, buildings that were massive and elaborate, but nevertheless looked as hollow and impermanent as the creampuff fantasies of a world's fair, something indescribably dreary . . . and—yes, . . . *temporary,* about the whole place" (HFG, 447). But, ironically reversing expectations again, Aiken suggests that at the city's source, giving it life and whatever stable identity it has, is the paradox of the great river, ever changing but changeless in its flow. Drawn initially to its energy, men built their mansions and commercial monuments in an effort to organize and harness the strength. Attracted to some sort of promise in its unbroken resources, they sought to bind the river in an effort to make permanent the city's energy. Yet the procedure threatens the very idea of promising energy that first was attractive—"an immense creative giving . . .

and mankind beside it become as spiritually empty as the locust, and as parasitic" (HFG, 449). And Aiken suggests, doubly iron- ically, that when we finally see the city clearly it is evident that the "wilderness [will] come back—the wilderness had never really been defeated here" (HFG, 447) despite the domestic forms. Yet to an extent the river itself, source of so much of this wilderness, did and still does submit itself to human forms and rituals, providing the very foundations for a sense of order, place, and permanence.

They were all silent, watching the changing land, the land which now rapidly divulged itself in long, parallel hollows, as if at some time chan- neled. . . .
    "Ah," said Noni, "the Mississippi—the father of waters—now we can go home!" . . .
    ". . . I feel as if in the twinkling of an eye—or while, in fact, we were crossing the bridge—my soul had shot under water . . . even into the Gulf of Mexico, and back again. And now it *belongs* to me...." (HFG, 446)

Like tide marks left by the sea, lines of gray and withered flotsam . . . marked the many levels at which during the winter the great river had stood. An enormous beach; against which the dark water slid with sleepy power, the brown eddies moving swiftly downstream as they coiled sparkling in the sunlight. A little way upstream, two river boats rotted at a landing stage. . . . Noni dipped her hand in the water. . . .
    "Now I'm baptized, Blom, in this continent." (HFG, 448)

At the geographic and symbolic center of his novel Aiken seems to invite his readers to realize that they can perceive energy and order in their environment without letting one cancel or diminish the other. He has slowed for a moment the language of movement, controlling it without rendering it sterile or static. The energy felt in the images of the river's sleepy strength and eddying motion—the occasional swift, downstream rush—is the source of a ritual harmony, but clearly it cannot be manacled. Man, the adventuring and domesticating animal, can succeed only if, allowing his two impulses to support each other, he meets natural force with sympathy, inviting—not commanding—order out of chaos.

The last leg of the trip begins abruptly, as if the travellers have fallen over the edge of the known world after being suddenly released from a state of suspended animation in St. Louis: "And in fact the train had now become positively suicidal. It was at last rushing downhill, hurling itself precipitately down the mountain sides . . . lurching in the breakback fashion around screaming bends" (HFG, 462-63). It is a nightmare world of distorted shapes and sounds, of familiar objects rendered terrifyingly abnormal by an intense alliterative accumulation of unusual adjectives and verbs. The language seethes with barely controlled motion, and the eye and tongue trip over the clotted descriptions while the mind recoils from images of the malevolent things that inhabit the dark place:

And not the least the alien sky, with those gizzard-colored thunderheads already piling up . . . and not least the smells of these filthy little streets . . . the stinking green-gray water that flowed down the gutters. . . .

He had been walking a long time; exploring with an indifferent eye, the sights of Cuernavaca. . . . The fernlike trees were so interlaced across [the gorge] that one thought of course it must be very shallow; only when one looked a second time did one glimpse—far below—and with a sudden contraction of the heart—tiny rocks and ripples in the filtered sunlight, knotted roots on the dank sides of the narrow little canyon, and the sinister suckers of the creepers, venomous and dark, hanging down hundreds of feet in search of a foothold. (HFG, 463-64)

The approaching storm had formed an immense purple-black canopy over the city. . . . [H]undreds of birds were quarreling and screaming, darting to and fro . . . meaninglessly. (HFG, 466)

The disorientation is as much a product of the agonizing realization that we are getting closer to Noni's death as it is the result of being and feeling in a foreign place. Yet it remains clear that Aiken insists upon the value of dislocation of body and mind, despite its terrifying implications, as a means of recognizing the interconnectedness of human experiences—the inseparability of multiplicity and pattern, permanence and impermanence. To die in an alien place is horrifying, yet it is worse to die without having submitted honestly and openly to the encounter with life that comes from confronting the unknown. In a painterly scene of dangerously clashing images—sun and ice together, fierce vermillion against a radiant sky, a nightmare version of Eden transformed—Aiken offers a sense of renewal. Like Coleridge's "miracle of rare device, / A sunny pleasure-dome with caves of ice,"⁵ which one seems to hear echoed, the promise is realized in the momentary conjoining of contraries.

> And the indifferent violence of this night [Noni] would herself, also— gratefully, and with delight—have praised. Just the sort of fruitful and unforeseen counterpoint, nature's wild multiplicity, which she had always passionately loved! . . . And the lightning, too.... [T]he whole sky was quivering with it: and against this palpitant radiance came unceasingly the fierce downward stroke of vermilion or violet. . . .
>
> When he emerged on to the verandah, it was to face a world which over night had been brilliantly re-created: everything flashed and sparkled: in the dazzling east, once more visible, the great volcano sunned its shoulders of ice. (HFG, 470-71)

Despite the clarity of Aiken's theme of discovery the novel's ending is not without ambiguities. Aiken's response to the fact of death is unflinchingly honest. Death is shockingly final—frightening and frustrating to the survivors. We cannot help but feel with Blom after Noni's heart attack that "just for an instant . . . it was all an outrage . . . meaningless" (HFG, 471). The last sentences of the novel sicken us with the sense of having suddenly awakened with Blom to find ourselves lost: "He began shaking his head from side to side, slowly. . . . He . . . wanted to laugh out of pure misery. 'And Christ,' he thought . . . 'Christ, but I'm a long way from home!'" (HFG, 472). And yet if we have read *A Heart for the Gods of Mexico* carefully the feeling will indeed be "just for an instant," for we feel—with as much certainty as possible in a world that refuses reduction to a simple pattern—that "home" is a place of the mind as well as a physical place; Blom— and the reader—have discovered and defined their essential domestic places in the very process of separation.

If *A Heart for the Gods of Mexico* carries Aiken's characters
away from home in order to suggest, finally, the interconnectedness of domestic and adventurous experiences, Aiken's last novel,
Conversation: or Pilgrims' Progress (1940) achieves much the
same result without displacement. Just as *A Heart* is Aiken's on
the road novel, *Conversation* is his "sinfonia domestica" (WU, 20
May 1939), exploring relationships while literally opening, progressing, and closing in the same limited space.

South Yarmouth. . . . Action, 24 hours, in four long sections—a quarrel
between husband and wife, non stop, but with interludes of all the
minor domestic diurnal occupations—dishes, meals, baths, w.c.'s, people, plumbing, etc. . . . The quarrel gradually increases in openness
and intensity . . . and reaches its natural anticlimax in bed at the end.
Thassall. There is of course as you see no plot—the thing stands or falls
by virtue of its sheer realism, or not . . . and in moments of mild lunacy I
think the thing may even be by way of being a domestic classic. (WU, 20
May 1939)

For all its fixed forms, however, the novel's sweep seems to be
among Aiken's largest. Without moving his characters from
home and hearth, Aiken manages to make the novel include not
just other places, but other times as well. Juxtaposing long quotations from the pilgrim narrative *A Journal of the Pilgrims at Plymouth: Mourt's Relation* with the progressing domestic narrative
of Timothy Kane (Tip), Enid, and their daughter Buzzer, Aiken
provides for the reader a kind of stereoscopic vision—one eye
focusing on the New England present, the other on the New England past. The impingement of historical moments on our consciousness makes us feel that this is not simply a tale of family
habits and crisis, but that in fact it reflects something elemental in
the American psyche that is as old as the earliest narratives of
exploration, and involves many of the challenges, uncertainties,
and discoveries connected with the exploration of unknown
worlds.

The sub-title refers incidentally to the fact that I've interleaved the four
sections with page-long quotes from the Journal of the Pilgrims, pas-

sages describing Cape Cod, indian huts, etc.—a rather nice device, making a . . . little ironic commentary. And the cape cod background is
given considerable value in the text as well, so that one feels that this
family row is taking place on a stage from which the pilgrims and indians have only just departed. (WU, 20 May 1939)

The opening chapter of *Conversation* begins, unlike many
exploration narratives, with a landing rather than with a leave-
taking. A quote from *Mourt's Relation,* which provides a touchstone of moods and emotion against which we are invited to measure the ensuing action, suggests that with the uncertainties of an
ocean voyage now over we are about to step forth for the first
time into a land of plenty and promise:

> . . . and after many difficulties in boisterous storms, at length, by
> God's providence . . . we espied land, which we deemed to be Cape
> Cod. . . . And the appearance of it much comforted us . . . it caused us
> to rejoice together and praise God that had given us once again to see
> land. And . . . upon the 11th November we came to an anchor in the bay,
> which is a good harbour and pleasant bay . . . compassed about to the
> very sea with oaks, pines, juniper, sassafras, and other sweet wood. . . .
> There was the greatest store of fowl that ever we saw. . . . [*Mourt's Rela-
> tion*] (C, 475)[6]

Yet this is to be as much a journey of exploration as any we have
read. The reader, upon landing in the New England countryside
some three hundred years after the first pilgrims, will indeed discover a place of promise. He will also discover a place of failed
promises, where the constrictions of social forms—so much a
legacy of the attitudes of the community-minded pilgrims themselves, who banded together against the dangers of the American
wilderness—threaten to blight the promise for Timothy Kane
and his family. In some respects this New England was—and still
is—a paradise of snakes. Yet, though the threat to the novel's
characters is most pronounced in terms of tensions related to
social forms, the reader will discover in this journey of inner
exploration that at the level of domestic social relationships, freedom and the energies and the hopes it produces still exist.
    Aiken introduces his readers to a world of immeasurable

promise by presenting impressions of place seen through a child's eye. The shock of freshness and the sense of wonder are juxtaposed without comment alongside the descriptions of pilgrims arriving in a new world. Aiken seems to suggest that the sense of mystery, still inherent in the place itself when it is seen without a grid of established social expectations, reflects the first wondrous perceptions of the place. In the modern instance, though, he would have us understand that the wonder is not simply in the fact of place itself; it is in large part the result of a creative giving in the domestic relationship of father and daughter that permits this sort of imaginative sense of life in all things. As Timothy Kane readies his child for bed, both adult and child—and eavesdropping reader—discover an energized world of fluid forms in which all of nature becomes suddenly animated.

With a child's insatiable curiosity, Buzzer responds vitally to her environment—to its sounds, sights, and inevitable changes. Even while she is beginning to comprehend the world as "reasonable" in adult terms, she is drawing her father from his adult's world of well-established reasonable answers into a world that seems to demand imaginative answers to elemental questions. It is clear that the "facts" will not speak to the sense of wonder implicit in the questions; the exchange between father and child suggests just how inadequate neatly formulated responses to environmental forces would be. As one question leads to another, the sense of the inexplicability of life-as-we-find-it grows more pronounced:

"Tirra-lirra, tirra-loo, tirra-lirra, tirra-lee—"
    "That doesn't make sense, daddy."
    "Neither it does. But what does it matter? . . . And now then, young woman, how about getting out of that there bath. It's late! Look how late it is! It's autumn! The leaves are falling off the trees! . . ."
    "Why do the leaves come off the trees, daddy?" . . .
    ". . . Once a year the trees all get very tired, and very sleepy, and they want to go to bed. . . .
    ". . . [S]o what do they do? They do just exactly what *you* do, they take off their clothes."

"And the leaves are their clothes! But *we* don't have leaves for clothes, daddy!" . . .

"And then do the trees go to sleep?"

She put her hands on the window sill, to look again at the falling of the leaves, automatically raised them as he lowered the little nightgown over the curled head, and worked them skilfully through the sleeves, the face with primmed mouth once more emerging in triumph, like a seal from a wave.

"The trees, bless their hearts, go to sleep. All winter they just dream and rest, exactly, for all the world, as if they were in their beds. After all, you have *flower* beds, you know!"

"Ho-ho—and who'd like to sleep in a flower bed! Not me!"

He turned her around, opened the door, smacked her small bottom, guided her toward the hall with a firm finger planted in the middle of her back.

"Well, off to your own, then. . . . Quick! March!" (C, 475-76)

In the quiet moments after the exchange, Tip's own creative energy seems to continue flowing, his eye both perceiving and creating his environment. Though his imaginative response is harsher than the child's, it is in motion in much the same way, receptive to the confusions of the natural world. Despite his sense of failure as a painter—"Impotence, impotence—the hand powerless to shape the actual, the vision powerless to purify its own shafts of light" (C, 478)—Kane, charged by the creativity of the father-daughter rituals, feels and represents the interconnectedness of natural shapes and colors.

The last of the autumn sunlight slanted across the unfinished picture which stood on the easel—the colors jumped out . . . glowed, he felt himself flowing into that shape of ruin, that shape of an old barn on a tangled hill, amongst wild grass, wild lilacs, wild apple trees. (C, 478)

Tip faces honestly his inability to catch the energy with fixed forms.

Everything flowed into everything else, flowed out of everything else. . . . The world was always thus getting away from him, going too fast, whizzing off before he had time to shape it. . . . It was always as if he were trying desperately to get hold of it before it was too late. (C, 494-95)

Yet Aiken also makes clear that to the extent that Tip does "get hold" of the flow, it is often in actions related simply to establishing or sustaining the careful forms of a domestic world (with his daughter, but more generally as well) rather than in the shaping performance of his art. Kane resembles the first domesticating settlers, who also sought to tame the wilderness, as the interspersed quotes from *Mourt's Relation* tell us: to find "acres, fit for the plough" (C, 503); to build "houses . . . with long young sappling trees, bended, and both ends stuck into the ground . . . made round, like unto an arbour" where "one might stand and go upright in them" (C, 533). Kane has sought in the country a place to build literally and symbolically his abode. Like the earliest European settlers who found "boughs and bushes . . . hills and valleys, which tore our very armour in pieces" (C, 503), Kane has been made vulnerable, at least symbolically, by the country environment in which he seeks to dwell. And like the pilgrims, he has discovered—with his "armour" somewhat stripped away— that although the place, even with villages built upon it, may be harsh and forbidding, one can find an excellent spot to sow a domestic garden. Its formal beauty will capture with its very order some of the dazzling energy and beauty implicit in the unknowable and dangerous wild place itself. Yet the general domestic impulse, if misapprehended and misdirected, can lead to the death and destruction of all energy and growth and change, leaving the earth "itself looking dead and frozen, with its cold barnacles of houses . . . look[ing] like . . . a vast skull; or worse still, like an exposed and frozen brain" (C, 497).

. . . towards noon warm and fair weather. The birds sang in the woods most pleasantly. At one o'clock it thundered, which was the first we heard in that country. It was strong and great claps, but short; but after an hour it rained very sadly till midnight . . . . This day some garden seeds were sown . . . . [*Mourt's Relation*] (C, 551)

But time, in such moonlight . . . poured . . . flowed . . . one elemental tree tip to another, frosted with pure light—the creeping diagonal of dense shadow . . . the slow tide of silver mounting up the still slope of a shingled roof, and then pouring soundlessly away over the rooftree to leave it again in primordial darkness . . . terrifying. . . .

His shovel rose and fell; cutting. . . . Cold roots, cold soil, cold sand—his hands, pressing down the lilac roots . . . took on something of the coarse violence of earth. . . . [T]he upright lilacs began to look like a hedge along the wall above the lane, it was beginning at last to be impressive. . . . Yes, already the garden had changed, was changing. It had suddenly become organized. (C, 497)

[H]e was engulfed abruptly in an astonishing silence. The crickets, all but a few, were still, now—their slower *zeek—zeek—zeek—zeek* was merely the moonlight made audible, the thin threnody of the moonlight itself. Peace be with you. (C, 499)

What a magnificent sense Aiken gives of the wilderness and the domestic experience giving way one to the other, in a kind of ongoing process that combines the continually shifting promise and pain, beauty and terror, implicit in the possibilities of both restriction and freedom. With the objects of the scene both diaphanous and tactile, the colors both sharp and shimmering in the moonlight, the wild and the orderly seem to partake of each other endlessly. It is, as Aiken suggests, a "mystery," "a nice word, and a very important one . . . as big as a hollowed-out mountain" (C, 476).

Still, the novel offers another mystery, just as great, for our consideration. We are invited to observe how quickly all the shaping energy implicit both in creating domesticity and in dealing with a relatively undomesticated place can be swept away when domestic forms are substituted for the essential domestic relationships that led to the invention of the forms in the first place. The insistence upon patterns of behavioral rituals without concern for the importance of the creative relationships that were once part of the rituals themselves too often leads to a sort of sterility, which dulls responsiveness to all possibilities of life and leaves form itself empty of meaning.

The ostensible focus for Aiken's portrayal of domestic discord is Enid Kane's worry about losing community approval and support. The "dreary little village" (C, 491), which she sometimes despises but must make peace with, clearly frowns upon Tip's recent friendship with Jim Connor, a somewhat unsavory outsider who as a professional big-city thief is a constant irritant to the local population. Yet the problem is only a symptom of the marital difficulties of the Kanes. Aiken presents a portrait of people who have not ceased to care for each other, but who have lost a means of expressing their affection. The actions of Enid and Tip, who are forever bickering about small violations of social form, have begun to be determined by behavioral codes, rather than by mutual responsiveness to changing individual needs.

The environment for both Tip and Enid is electric with the tension of constant disharmony. The fractured images that Aiken uses to describe the disintegrating relationship bear little resemblance to the fluid metaphors of creation we have already encountered. The Kane home becomes simply a collection of discrete objects—"Enid's empty chair," a "disordered studio," a closed bedroom door (C, 502-3). It fills with discordant sounds— a "gramaphone [that] squawked and ran down," "Enid's iron, in the kitchen, [that] clashed on its metal rest" (C, 509)—or becomes terrifyingly empty of all noise—"the house [is] silent" (C, 503). All conversation seems fixed on such issues as when to fix the cesspool, who is to prepare lunch, and whether to hold supper, or on the increasingly sore subject of when Tip is to reject Jim Connor. Given the circumstances of failed communication, the obsessive attention to the forms of household activities often seems bitterly ironic—Enid admitting Tip to her bedroom, for instance, simply to have him stack the laundered shirts on her bed (C, 552), or Enid suggesting during a quick verbal skirmish that Tip can find his own "cold tongue . . . in the icebox" for lunch (C, 524).

The language of communication becomes jagged and brittle; words and physical gestures drive a wedge between the Kanes. By the end of chapter two, husband and wife seem strangers. As if existing on different sides of a gulf that has opened between them, glimpsing each other indistinctly or piecemeal, they shout angrily across the void, gesticulating with awkward motions like badly made puppets.

The bitter words, bitterer than somehow he had expected them to be, were addressed to the vanishing green back, . . . the self-consciously upright head. . . . He was sitting rigid in his chair, the knife and fork held hard in his hands. . . . [H]e must quickly find something . . . for his hands to do, something violent. . . . (C, 529)

She stood still, her hands still held oddly up before her . . . [and] he was aware as if through his back that she had not moved . . . her whole attitude one of helpless rage. (C, 530)

Turning too quickly, lest he give her time to answer, he tripped over the hall rug, stumbled, kicked it from him violently. . . . And then in his haste to retrieve himself, miscalculating in the dark struck his right shoulder, painfully, against the doorjamb of the dining room. How disgusting—how grotesque. (C, 556)

The actions and emotions are disorienting, having the impact of "last-minute comedy that turns a tragedy into a farce" (C, 556). But perhaps even more discomforting for the reader than the sense that characters can be dehumanized by the failure of domestic relationships is the sense that when domestic relationships break down so too does all spatial coherence and harmony. Aiken makes clear once again that the risks and comforts of place depend not so much on external circumstances themselves as on modes of perception, states of mind. When Tip and Enid cease to communicate, their environments dissolve. The home they have made together, to help keep out the dangers of formless and unprotected open spaces, seems rather to lock in the most terrifying aspects of openness. We find ourselves observing along with Tip "how extraordinarily a silence can put *distance* between people, or turn a small house into a big one—as now, for instance, with positively an Atlantic Ocean spreading its screaming wastes between the studio and the kitchen" (C, 557). Aiken seems to be hearkening back to his opening quotation from *Mourt's Relation,* reminding us that, although in some ways we have travelled far in the more than three hundred years since the pilgrims' Cape Cod landing, building our communities in the wilderness, we are, without the creating energy of imaginative relationships, as much as ever still voyaging in trackless waters amidst "boisterous storms" (C, 475).

When Tip and Enid finally do have a complete blow-up followed by "a *conversation*" (C, 567) near the novel's end, it is a dialogue that reaffirms for both the importance in their relationship of "imaginative sympathy" (C, 561) and concludes with the promise of new life—an "omen" half-jokingly mentioned of the birth of "a son" (C, 575). Aiken is suggesting the triumph of human caring. It is a victory that seems to suggest a link with the spirit of the American past itself, as Aiken juxtaposes the storms and promises of the present moment with the pilgrim narratives of exploration. As the last entry from *Mourt's Relation* indicates, the times of "strong and great claps" of thunder and hard rain are also times for the sowing of seeds (C, 551).

Aiken's last novel makes no effort, then, to deny the difficulties of living in a precarious environment that stimulates human hopes for order and creative imagining at the same time that it threatens them with sterility and chaos. *Conversation* suggests, simply, that men and women cannot be dominated or defeated by natural or man-made external forces, unless they choose to be. Both promise and terror are, finally, as much matters of mind and will as of physical place. The human spirit, capable of imaginative giving, but too self-bound to be able to manage it much of the time, will continue to seek and to falter. Men and women will explore on their voyaging the continually merging pleasures and pains of domestic order and discord, and the harmony and chaos of the adventures that take place at the frontiers of the land and of the mind. What Conrad Aiken gives us in *A Heart for the Gods of Mexico* and *Conversation,* as he begins to re-explore his American terrain in detail, is a sensitive and intelligent appraisal of what it means to be human.

11 The Unconquerable Ancestors

"Mayflower," "The Kid," "Hallowe'en"

With the publication of *A Heart for the Gods of Mexico* and *Conversation,* Aiken succeeded in firmly mapping the broad outlines of an exploration of the American terrain as place and as metaphor; over the next decade he steadily filled in the map, giving his attention repeatedly (though not exclusively) to the nature of his American experience. As he tells it, what steered his imagination during this time of relocation was the heightened sense of ancestry that accompanied his return to New England. "I found," Aiken says simply, "that my ancestral roots claimed me."[1]

> The ancestors, the ancestors, the unconquerable ancestors, whose tongues still spoke so clearly, whose hands still reached so unmistakably. . . . Each bud, and then each leaf, each flower, taking up the precious pattern, repeating it; perhaps only with the most infinitesimal variation, the slightest imaginable, and probably accidental, accretion, of one's own. (U, 45)

And yet, attention to Aiken's works written during these years suggests that the process of reclamation of and by the homeland was a complex one, involving more than one idea of ancestry and taking the poet down different paths of discovery. "Mayflower" (1945), "The Kid" (1947), and "Hallowe'en" (1949), three central works of the period, mark in particular the intricacies of Aiken's "discovery and acceptance of America" and of "his own ghosts in it" (U, 336).[2]

"Mayflower," as the title suggests, is a poem of both departure and arrival. It is Aiken's bridge into the new world, identifying the freshness and immediacy of new experience and affirming too a link of old with new as part of perception. Ancestry here seems more a matter of cultural connectedness than a personal feeling of belonging, and yet the discovered ancestral presences, however generalized, offer comfort amidst the confusion of the unfamiliar.

Having arrived on the new world's shore, Aiken discourses with the past, extending the techniques we have already seen used in *Conversation* of mingling living voices with quotes and echoes of voices from a long-gone time. Aiken's speaker in "Mayflower" demands our full attention with his first word: "Listen" (SP, 236). And if we give it, we will hear and learn the ways "the ancient voices hail us from the farther shore" of new world leave-taking, of older times and cultures that are, in fact, continuous with our own. The voices of Aiken's literary godfathers "Will and Ben" (SP, 237)—Shakespeare and Jonson—linger on. And in the normal vocabulary men use to record their immediate experiences, we recognize the names of things carried from generation to generation.

"Mayflower" flows with sound and speech as the poet experiences "the New England spring" (SP, 236). The presence of the past is felt immediately in the imagined "cries and farewells . . . and the praying" of "devout [pilgrim] fathers," and in the vividly onomatopoetic diction that helps to set the scene, marking the clangor of "the hawser falling," the "weeping on the quayside" (SP, 236). The assemblage of sounds, which establishes the vitality of the experience of the past in the present, is given more formal, historical resonance as well when Aiken, having cast the moment in the mind's eye, lifts passages into his poem from *Mourt's Relation*, the pilgrim narrative journal he used so pointedly in *Conversation*. The formal language of the record, written with an eye toward both posterity and providence, and the concrete, descriptive images registered by the poet's senses energize and support one another. Together they inform both poet and reader of the design of permanence-in-change stamped on the face of things.

The controlled excitement of the pilgrims—who "by God's providence," "by break of day espied / land which we deemed to

be Cape Cod" and which "caused us to rejoice together and
praise God, / seeing so goodly a land, and wooded to the brink of
the sea" (SP, 236)—is indeed very different from nature's intense
voices, so alive for the sense-aware poet in his New England present. Observing his immediate surroundings, Aiken discovers
almost apocalyptic transformations of life. Inanimate objects act
as if with sentience: "the quick plough breaks dust," while frogs
and fish are anthropomorphized and even sunlight seems
"altered" by cycles of growth and renewal as "seagulls speak,"
ale-wives run, and the "new snake sleeps in altered light" (SP,
236-37). The noisy moment surrounds us:

the pinkwinks shrill, the pinkwinks trill,
crying from the bog's edge to lost Sheepfold Hill.
Spring, spring, spring, spring, they cry,
water voice and reed voice,
. . . .
. . . And on his log,
the whip-poor-will shrieks and thumps in the bright
    May-morning fog.

                                        (SP, 236-37)

Yet the poet's receptivity to the vital moment is not separable
from his discovered sense of himself as an inheritor of things
seen, of ways of seeing and communicating.

Yes: the ancient voices speak once more,
. . . .
their spring, still living, now
. . . .

Three hundred years of snow and change,
the Mermaid voices growing lost and strange;
. . . .
Yet not lost wholly:
in deed, in charter, and in covenant sweetly kept,
. . . .
and the ballad's melancholy.
. . . .

sung at maying, sung at haying,
shouted at husking to the fiddle's playing,
. . . .
And in the names kept too: sorrel and purslane,
ground-ivy, catnip, elecampane,
. . . .

Each child set out and tended his own tree,
to each his name was given. Thus, they still live, still see:
Mercy, Deborah, Thankful, Rufus and Amanda Clark,
trees that praise sunlight, voices that praise the dark.

(SP, 236-38)

"All's here" for the poet, "all's kept, for now / spring brings back the selfsame apple bough / that braved the sea three hundred years ago" (SP, 240). No longer exiled twice over but a traveller returned to discover himself a part of an intricate continuum, Aiken has crossed in "Mayflower" the threshold of his now not so "alien coast" (SP, 240). He sees "in the many-voiced country lane / . . . the fields of poverty grass and clover."

world without end to love and have it,
bee-blossom heart to love and live it,
this holy land, our faith itself. . . .

(SP, 240)

As Aiken tells it in *Ushant,* "the little mayflower poem" provided release "from inhibitory checkings" (U, 337). And in freeing the poet from insecurities, from doubts of belonging to the American scene, the poem seems to have provided Aiken with a comfortable starting point for further exploration of the new world experience he was setting out to rediscover in his middle years. He had established, for the moment, a sense of the basic continuity of new and old that affirms the particularity of each experience and yet suggests too the interweaving of past and present in a process of mutual definition. Aiken could turn now to explore more completely the "newness" of the new world experience, concentrating on his role as inheritor of attitudes that he defined as especially American.

Broadening and depersonalizing the notion of ancestral inheritance in his next important poem, "The Kid," Aiken concentrated on a special ancestral line whose largeness makes clear the poet's intention of offering

a sort of spiritual history of the U S (old Blackstone, and Anne Bradstreet, and Boone and Crevecoeur and Thoreau and Appleseed and the Quaker martyrs and Kit Carson and Billy the Kid and then Melville and Willard Gibbs and the Adams brothers in starlight (Brooks and Henry) (all ending of course with Emily Dickinson?)?? the "Kid" idea as the American eponymous hero, whether as pioneer of the inward or outward wilderness. (SL, 274)[3]

"The Kid" takes for its subject nothing less than a vision of the American national experience in which newness and uncertainty nurtured elastic language, produced varieties of geographic directions of exploration and settlement, and helped define the shape of groups of people as well as of the individual. Americans, as historian Daniel Boorstin has observed,

were not men moving ever *toward* the west, but men ever moving *in* the west. The churning, casual, vagrant, circular motion around and around was as characteristic of the American experience as the movement in a single direction.[4]

And Aiken portrays the new wanderer perfectly, offering a history of the tantalizing, traditional figure of the loner "who sought freedom and privacy in the 'wide open spaces,' or the physical conquest of an untamed continent, and those others, early and late, who were to struggle for it in the darker kingdoms of the soul" (CP, 1033). But he provides, too, a view of the broader spirit of the American frontier as it was embodied in clusters of transients.

Further, "The Kid" dares to suggest what our self-serious literature too often overlooks: that at the foundation of our most solemn American myths, humor and high seriousness are joined. As Aiken wrote to his friend John Gould Fletcher, "The Kid" is often *"light in tone,* dares a little to be *fun* . . . eschews the portentous, declines to be rigid or pseudo-intellectual or Kierkegaardian or solemn, cuts corners, simplifies, and rollicks its way in carefree octosyllabic couplets as apparently innocent as a backwoods ballad" (SL, 276). In offering his combinations of tone, of high-poetic diction and varieties of slang, of vigorous tall tales and gentle or crude songs of the people, Aiken is expressing his concern with an ambiguity that determines much of the transiency and that defined much of the comedy and the heroism of the new world wilderness experience.[5]

The poem, seeking to express the essence of Aiken's "always restless, always moving on" (SP, 219) spiritual ancestors, is laced with deliberate ambiguities. Aiken begins with the prototypically American figure of William Blackstone, who found his "untrodden kingdoms in the minde" (SP, 226). Following various mythic-historical incarnations of this wilderness explorer, the "eponymous hero" called the "Kid," we discover that even seemingly simple definitions of persons and places are impossible. For example, when we try to answer fairly straightforward questions about the "Kid" in general—"Who saw the Kid when he rose?" (SP, 220); "Who heard that lad leap down?" (SP, 220); "Who bore witness?" (SP, 222)—we realize that the "Kid" and the places he passes through can only be understood as mutually defining.

In rendering early impressions of the "Kid" and the land, Aiken gathers a multitude of poetic effects into a small space, crowding together internal rhymes, slant rhymes, assonance, consonance, alliteration, and an assemblage of onomatopoetic images. To "witness" seems suddenly an active rather than a passive mode of perception. And as we observe both traveller and natural witnesses, we are also drawn to active response by the energy of the language. In that sense we share in the process of definition. While we listen and look, a tongue-twisting catalogue of names, things, and places swells into a song of greeting that affects all our senses, enabling us to comprehend and participate in the experience of "moving on." Like a compressed geography or natural history lesson, the list reminds us anew of the existence of what may be familiar and enables us to conjure up the unfamiliar: "And rivers: rivers with their proud hosanna: / Chattahoochee: Tallahassee: Susquehanna / Savannah, high-yaller, and Arkansas, red" (SP, 223).

The poem provides as well a crowded parade of local references and colloquial, informal, or semiformal identifications of things. The "bullbriar patch," "groundhog," "cunning 'possum,'" "hummingbird moth in the scuppernong blossom," "hoarse Monomoy," "Grizzly," "longhorn," "Buffalo spine," "tumbleweed blowing" (SP, 221-222), all hear the "Kid's" approach, know him, admire him. These are, of course, the "Kid's" names for things in the untrodden kingdoms singing back to him in praise. Gaining and giving identity, he is "hailed" and "farewelled" (SP, 223) by the noise and activity of nature's constantly changing shape, by the flow of water, and by the "heat-song" (SP, 224) and "beast-cry" (SP, 224) of wild animals of all kinds and sizes. The "Kid" and his surroundings are perpetually taking form one from the other:

They caught his hymn as it fell to the sea
from condor's shadow and sugarpine-tree:
of might in singleness. . . .
> (SP, 223)

He turned to the land: forgot his name: Hector
changing and changeless went and came: St. John de
dreamed blood-knowledge as he slept in nature: Crèvecoeur
sucked blood-knowledge from the blood of the creature . . .
heartbeat probed in the heartbeat's place. . . .
> (SP, 229)

Ambiguities are compounded. Aiken's ubiquitous spiritual ancestor, both a man and more, is at once elusive and substantial. Like an elemental force, he rises with the sun and "rid[es] the bridled and fire-bright Beast" (SP, 220); seeming to command all

space, he "span[s] / wide water as only a rainbow can" (SP, 221).
From the force of his godlike fist comes "the lightning stroke, /
the double thunder and a puff of smoke" (SP, 222). Yet he is a
builder and a planter too, responsive to his world in the limited
ways a man can be, shaping it with the tools at his disposal.

He . . . laid axe to root: John Chapman
packed his knapsack with the seed of fruit:
· ·
framed a corncrib, and plowed up a field,
planted his corn and brought it to yield. . . .
                                        (SP, 229)

The "Kid" seems both a prime mover—"westward, seaward,
he drew the horizon"—and a being whose actions are determined
by external circumstances—"following the Sioux who followed
the bison" (SP, 221). As a man he is capable of a selfless apprecia-
tion of the possibilities of the wild: "Lord, lend me wisdom,
Lord, let me dream: / spent in thy heart was this sunshine day"
(SP, 229). But he can be merely arrogant and self-serving in his
response as well:

Said Tidewater Johnny to Bluewater Johnny,
you got to go west if you want to make money,
we built up the cities and filled them with people,
· ·
and the cities are pretty, but the forest is best. . . .
                                        (SP, 229-30)

Even the "Kid's" noble "hymn" of seasons and change often
sounds like little more than a folksy squawk, as Aiken juxtaposes
majestic visions with doggerel ballads interpolated into the
poem:

I'm away, I'm away, I'm away to the west,
· ·
my pa he can curse, my ma she can cry,
they'll all forgive me in the sweet by-and-by,

I come from heaven and to heaven I'll go,
but what's in between I'm a wantin' to know!
                                        (SP, 222)

The noble vision seemingly offers no truer glimpse of the "Kid"
than the low or comic view does. This is the lesson implicit in
realizing, with the help of the poet's ironic subject and image
rhyme, that the "Kid" who leaps down "over the night hard hoof-
beats pounding" (SP, 220), "his hair like fire and his eyes like ice; /
and a pinto pony, a wing of flame, / whinnying and gone as quick
as it came" (SP, 222), is a ghost to bemuse us, hovering over the
scene when two less-than-grand "Kids" enact their own version of
things and light out for the territories:

Said Catskill Johnny to Swannikan Johnny,
you fetch a horse and I'll find a pony,
we'll hitch Conestoga to a comet's tail
and hurry out west on the wilderness trail.
                                        (SP, 230)

What the deliberate ambiguities of Aiken's presentations suggest
is a portrait neither of men nor of gods, but rather a paradoxically *unambiguous* representation of a force whose extravagant
energies flow through the wide range of the American experience.
    The sometimes forced conjoining in "The Kid" of differing dic-
tions, actions, and visions has struck a sour note for a number of
Aiken's critics. Perhaps the bristliest, though typical enough, is
Frederick J. Hoffman:

The conception is faulty, the shifts of terms and of the grounds for
action, the almost frivolous slightness with which major important ideas
are treated, all mark *The Kid* as one of Aiken's conspicuous failures.[6]

And indeed the hoof-pounding rhythms can seem monotonous.
Too, the sudden juxtapositions of literary images, sufficiently
elevated to please the most cultivated connoisseur, with common

sing-songs, outrageous enough to bring a twinkle to the eye of most popular humorists, can be jarring. Still we would do well to recall that, as Herman Melville wrote, "there are some enterprises in which a careful disorderliness is the best method."[7] Neither consistently serious nor humorous, Aiken has tried—with considerable success—to provide something of a bridge between two traditional American literary reactions to the wilderness. As Aiken rightly sees, the two are linked by their responsiveness to energies released by the ambiguities of frontier life.

Aiken's singular achievement in "The Kid" is to offer a work that embraces the myths and dreams on which the western movement was based and the harsher, sometimes humorous realities of the frontier experience, without having one cancel the other. Walt Whitman, identified near the end of "The Kid" as one of the hero's late incarnations, once explained the expression of mythic and common experience in a way that we may use to offer our own "hail" and "farewell" to Aiken's accomplishment here. As if summing up the work of the poet-to-be, Walt Whitman wrote in *November Boughs,* a year before Aiken's birth:

Considering Language then as some mighty potentate, into the majestic audience-hall of the monarch ever enters a personage like one of Shakespeare's clowns, and takes position there, and plays a part even in the stateliest ceremonies. Such is Slang, or indirection, an attempt of common humanity to escape from bald literalism, and express itself illimitably, which in highest walks produces poets and poems, and doubtless in pre-historic times gave the start to, and perfected, the whole immense tangle of the old mythologies. For, curious as it may appear, it is strictly the same impulse-source, the same thing.[8]

Aiken himself seems to have understood better than anyone the crux of his problem with "The Kid." Indeed his next major poem, "Hallowe'en," goes a long way toward addressing it. The significant danger of the deliberate ambiguities in "The Kid," of its gathering, without sufficient distinctions, of so many different "Kids" under the general heading of spiritual ancestor, was the poet's loss of a centering, explicitly personal connection with his American inheritance. Although in "Mayflower" Aiken had generally realized his link with America, and in "The Kid" he had sweepingly explored an elemental American vision, he had not yet firmly located himself on the new continent by directly addressing his family roots. In "Hallowe'en," which complements the earlier explorations, the poet completes his discovery of his new-found old home by learning to comprehend and accept the presence of his own ghosts in it. For, as the poem makes clear in celebrating the days of the dead—All Saints' and All Souls' days—

in forgetting our obligations to the dead
we have neglected our living and our children's living
in neglecting our love
for the dead who would still live within us.

                                        (SP, 243)

In contrast to "The Kid," "Hallowe'en" raises ambiguities only to dispel them in the clarity of the poet's dialogue with his grandfather, William James Potter. Once more Aiken invites us to observe his new world, and once more we find it at times to be unsettlingly confused. Yet amidst the vagueness, sharply defined presences come forth. In the twilight settings of the poem, when the poet places us somewhere between waking and dreaming, forms and murmuring voices merge, pass into shadow, and reemerge as living images in a ceremony of remembering. With each ritual return, the intensity of ancestral presences and the sense of their world helps to define the poet's own world.

Aiken presents a kind of enchanted environment where it is difficult to measure the clear outlines of things, where hints of deep mysteries accumulate while words swell in rhythmic regularity and repetition:

The moon . . . lights her bonfire
behind Sheepfold Hill, old corpse-fire
blazing through oaktrees, the bone-fire
which, in forests, the priests called *ignis ossium.*

                                        (SP, 240)

Here speaker and reader tense with the anticipation of unusual occurrences. It is a tension both heightened and relieved by "the homeless" figures that "come to complain and to haunt" (SP, 241). For, paradoxically, the apparitions offer the only solidity to be found, compelling our attention to the pains of their displacement.

These figures demand an agony of recognition that, though disconcerting, is less damaging than ignorance. The intensity of their presence clearly invites responses that can begin a process of clarification and change, as grandfather and grandson, blending identities, exchange insights:

In the old time, the country,
these two days, these two holy days,
were devoted to the dead. . . .
. . . .
we went in and knelt among bones. And the bones
. . . .
joined in complaint and besought us
for prayers. . . .
. . . .

but now none remembers, . . .
. . . .
you come back to abuse and to haunt us,
you, grandfather . . . and the others:
to the forgetful house, yourselves not forgetful,
. . . .
you return once more to remind us.
. . . .
it is our ancestors and children who conspire against us
life unlived and unloved that conspires against us
our neglected hearts and hearths that conspire against us
. . . .

And the spirit, the unappeased houseless spirit,
whose dwelling should be in ourselves, those who inherit,
. . . .
homeward once more looks now for prayer and praise

to be with laurels blest
and in our breast
live out his due bequest of nights and days.

                    (SP, 241-43)

Any dwellings we are going to make for ourselves in a new world
must have rooms for the still-loved presences of our closest
ancestors; otherwise, lacking the solid foundation that a sense of
personal continuity offers, we will have failed, whatever our
efforts, to clear a place in the vast and ambiguous land.

    The conclusion of "Hallowe'en" brings us from endings full
circle to beginnings. Ritual death promotes rebirth, and for
Aiken it is a rebirth in memory, a fusion of ritual completion and
ritual initiation that, in affirming the interconnectedness of
human lives past and present, illuminates for us all the ambiguous
places in which we live:

O you who made magic
under an oak-tree once in the sunlight
translating your acorns to green cups and saucers
for the grandchild mute at the tree's foot,
and died, alone, on a doorstep at midnight
· ·
dear scarecrow, dear pumpkin-head!
who masquerade now as my child, to assure
the continuing love . . .
and the heart and the hearth and the wholeness—
it was so, it is so, and the life so lived
shines this night like the moon. . . .

· ·
Rest: be at peace. It suffices to know and to rest.
For the singers, in rest, shall stand as a river
whose source is unending forever.

                    (SP, 245)

    "Not for nothing," then, as Aiken once wrote, "had been those
compulsory war years at the Cape Cod farmhouse, and the prolonged reimmersion in the ancestral scene" (U, 297). Secure in

Brewster (and later Savannah) at last and having firmly established in his work both a satisfying general and an intense personal response to American places and people, Aiken would choose, paradoxically, in "A Letter from Li Po" and "The Crystal," his major poems of the next decades, to speak from the voice of exile rather than arrival. Aiken once worried in *Ushant* that when

one felt at home, one would have no more to learn, or would have become so relaxed as to be no longer capable of learning; and one's very purpose for having come there at all, or a very important part of it, would be no longer valid. (U, 334)

As if to affirm that being "home" need not mean complacency, that he could still "take on the whole damned world"—even better for planting his creative energy in the rich soil in which he had uncovered ancestral roots—Aiken broadened the range of his final "longer philosophical meditations."9 He mingled American places with faraway locations, blending his own and ancestral voices with those of historical and legendary figures. But for now, in "Mayflower," "The Kid," and "Hallowe'en," Aiken had rediscovered his America, "in the delighted acknowledgment of one's debts, one's ties, one's roots, one's belongingness" (U, 337).

12 This Marriage of Text and Thing
"A Letter from Li Po" and "The Crystal"

In a 1964 *Atlantic Monthly* essay Aiken, aged seventy-five, engaged in a bit of retrospection, evaluating his present in relation to his past:

Eliot, as we all know, elected France and what was then "modern" French poetry and got this creative venom into his veins before the fortunes of World War I settled him in England. I myself preferred the English tradition and lived there many years because that seemed to me what I needed. Later, the fortunes of another war sent me back to America. . . . I should have remained there all the time.[1]

Yet "A Letter from Li Po" (1955) and "The Crystal" (1958),[2] the major poems illuminating Aiken's late writings, are anything but stay-at-home verses. "Li Po" powerfully conjures up the restless Chinese poet whose life's work seems a series of variations on the theme of the outsider's hardships of travel,[3] whereas "The Crystal" vividly recalls Pythagoras, whose break with the Samian tyrant Polycrates precipitated a move in old age from Samos to Croton.[4]

Aiken's attention to the wanderer at a time when the poet had himself essentially settled in seems less perplexing when we are reminded later in the *Atlantic Monthly* essay of the career-shaping lesson from Santayana that Aiken learned early and remembered late—"that poetry at its best and broadest must be philosophical, must have at its center some sort of world view, or *weltanschauung.*"[5] As Aiken had explained to Douglas Bridson:

I think it was [Santayana's] lectures on Goethe that most influenced me in the direction of becoming deliberately a philosophic poet. He himself stressed the value of the philosophic poet as providing a greater height from which to see things, and a greater space in which to spread them. (BBC II, 1)

Mixing the familiar with the unfamiliar, Aiken reconfirms for himself and for the reader that the poet is always an outsider in some sense. He is a wanderer even in known places, and yet at the same time he is a perceiver whose vision of wholeness in all things finally makes inappropriate the notion of spatial and temporal limit.

The poet's clear eye sees better than most the distinctness of things, but he is also more likely than most to recognize with William James that "in life distinct things can and do commune together every moment."[6] Peter Goffin explained the paradox in *The Realm of Art,* a book that Aiken tells us he found "brilliant" and "very suggestive" during the composition of "A Letter from Li Po" (CP, 1036):

The person who feels and appreciates things anew for himself, and who dares to declare himself in the face of the established and authoritative . . . system into which he happens to be born, is not only a rare person, he is also a social heretic. . . .
    . . . The most obvious, and literally outstanding, of these person-alities are the artists who produce what we call "fine" art.[7]

The true aim and purpose of civilization is the realization of nature *through* art, the realization of the elemental and latent harmony which is the moving equilibrium of life. It is the intelligent and intuitive orches-tration and performance of that given and basic harmony with ever increasing subtlety, distinction, and refinement. It is the conscious *artic-ulation* of life.[8]

"A Letter from Li Po" begins with a series of puzzles of iden-tity, setting, and theme, that move gradually toward solution as the reader is compelled not simply to perceive meaning as he reads but to bring it into being. As he does so, he becomes con-scious of the writer's controlling presence. That the epistle is very much a written artifact is clear in the syntactical convolutions and

verbal tensions of the early stanzas. Less obvious to the reader is
the knowledge that this is a letter "from" rather than "to" or
"about" Li Po. The poetic scene is vaguely set "Somewhere
beyond the Gorge" (SP, 245), where letter writer Li Po, presented
peculiarly enough in the third person rather than in the first person singular, "is gone, / looking for friendship" (SP, 245). The
voice that addresses the reader in this letter is certainly not in any
literal sense that of the tenth-century "banished Immortal."[9] In
fact, the information about the title figure that comes forth in
answer to the speaker's queries simply raises the level of uncertainty by presenting additional linguistic and factual indirec-
tions. The question "What was his light?" (SP, 245) is answered
only by the second query—offered with deliberately confusing
grammatical awkwardness—"of lamp or moon or sun?" (SP,
245). "What was his time?" only resolves into a riddle:

> Say that it was a change,
> but constant as a changing thing may be,
> from chicory's moon-dark blue down the taut scale
> to chicory's tenderest pink, in a pink field
> such as imagination dreams of thought.
>
> (SP, 246)

Aiken does not seek to recreate Li Po mimetically, or to give himself over to the poet's personae. Rather, he calls the reader's attention to the fact that what he has put before the reader is a thing
made of words that must be self-consciously read—pondered,
broken down, reassembled—thus making meaning in the recognition of the process of seeing as much as in things seen. Aiken is
identifying himself with Li Po in their shared role as verbal craft-
ers who both exhibit and compel the creating imagination. In this
way, Aiken manages simultaneously to place and displace his
reader in space and time, for what we discover in this celebration
of the art of poetry making is a picture neither of Li Po nor of
Conrad Aiken; yet it is one that straddles the times and places of
both in its sense of the essential oneness of identity of all such
makers:

to spell down the poem on her page,
. . . .
. . . is to assume
Li Po himself: as he before assumed
the poets and the sages who were his.
Like him, we too have eaten of the word:
with him are somewhere lost beyond the Gorge:
and write, in rain, a letter to lost children. . . .

(SP, 246)

Glimpses of poets' worlds ten centuries apart are clustered throughout the poem but are neither self-contained nor kept distinct. Li Po's world is established less with descriptive details than with echoes, paraphrases, and quotations from such poems as "I Am a Peach Tree," "The Silk Spinner," and "Chuang Chou and the Butterfly,"[10] which serve not only to render the environment but also to remind the reader that Li Po's world is a still-living presence and is boundless. Aiken refers, for example, to Li Po's poem about the Taoist philosopher Chuang Chou:

Li Po

allowed his autumn thoughts . . . to flow,
and, from the Gorge, sends word of Chouang's dream.
Did Chouang dream he was a butterfly?
Or did the butterfly dream Chouang? If so,
why then all things can change, and change again.

(SP, 249)

The lines have their parallel elsewhere in the poem in Aiken's own, somewhat Emersonian, contemplation:

We are the tree, yet sit beneath the tree,
among the leaves we are the hidden bird,
we are the singer and are what is heard.

(SP, 247)

The effect of such an overtone is to make the reader realize—in answer to such Aiken queries as "What is this 'world'?" (SP,

247)—that it is "Not Li Po's . . . alone" (SP, 247). And in response
to the question "What is this 'man'? How far from him is 'me'?"
(SP, 247), we recognize that "This 'I'" is the common identity of
"the master of the cadence" (SP, 249):

> this moving "I," this focal "I,"
> which changes, when it dreams the butterfly,
> into the thing it dreams of; liquid eye
> in which the thing takes shape, but from within
> as well as from without. . . .
>   (SP, 249)

"All Things" are "transform[ed] . . . to a hoop of flame, where-
through / tigers of meaning leap" (SP, 249), in an inherited living
"language never old and never new, / such as the world wears on
its wedding day" (SP, 249).

Aiken presents his own, twentieth-century Cape Cod world
with meticulous attention to naturalistic detail, yet he refuses to
allow his reader to give himself over completely to the reality of
the scene. With one eye directed to the things on Sheepfold Hill,
and the other to the written page itself, we become aware again of
reality being contrived and controlled for us:

> We climb the hill
> through bullbriar thicket and the wild rose, climb
> past poverty-grass and the sweet-scented bay
> scaring the pheasant from his wall, but can we say
> that it is only these, through these, we climb,
> or through the words, the cadence, and the rhyme?
>   (SP, 252)

As if in response to Aiken's rhetorical question "And in this
marriage of text and thing how can we know / where most the
meaning lies?" (SP, 252), we are discovering that "The landscape
and the language are the same. / And we ourselves are language
and are land" (SP, 254). People, places, family histories, and tradi-

tional literary ones are conjoined by the imagination of the artist who reads to us the leaves "that fill the Book of Change" (SP, 256):

> all is text, the immortal text,
> Sheepfold Hill the poem, the poem Sheepfold Hill,
> and we, Li Po, the man who sings, sings as he climbs,
> transposing rhymes to rocks and rocks to rhymes. . . .
>
> (SP, 252)

> How still
> the Quaker Graveyard, the Meeting House how still,
> where Cousin Abiel, on a night like this,
> now long since dead, but then how young, how young,
> scuffling among the dead leaves after frost
> looked up and saw the Wine Star, listened and heard
> borne from all quarters the Wind Wheel Circle word:
> the father within him, the mother within him, the self
> coming to self through love of each for each.
> In this small mute democracy of stones
> is it Abiel or Li Po who lies
> and lends us against death our speech?
> They are the same, and it is both who teach.
>
> (SP, 256)

According to Arthur Waley, who is quoting, paraphrasing, and interpreting Li Po, the Chinese poet

claims to have "seen the Greater Earth sharp and clear as in a mirror," and to have "revolved through space with the Wheeling Wind," that is to say, to have reached the stage of concentration called the "Wind Wheel Samadhi," in which the untethered mind wanders at will through space."[11]

The account might well serve to sum up Conrad Aiken's intention and achievement in "A Letter from Li Po." Rehearsing in old age the discoveries of his craft, writing a poem that is nothing so much as a poem about poetry making, he "brings back, to the all-remembering world, its ghosts, / borne from the Great Year on the Wind Wheel Circle" (SP, 256).

And they are here, Li Po and all the others,
our fathers and our mothers . . .

. . . .

        all mankind
and all it ever knew is here in-gathered,
held in our hands, and in the wind
breathed by the pines on Sheepfold Hill.
                (SP, 256)

    In "Li Po" Aiken discovered a kindred spirit whose achieve-
ment helped focus and enrich his own. In "The Crystal" he
employed Pythagoras as his exemplar figure, a creative thinker
whose theories on the nature of the cosmos, the human soul, and
mathematical form offered a more systematic model for summarizing Aiken's own artistic concerns. As Charles Seltman, a
source for much of Aiken's information, explained:

Heracleitus recognized that there can be no knowledge of that which is
in flux. Up to this point thinkers had been asking "what is Being?" From
now on, they found themselves obliged to ask also "what is Knowledge?"
    The answer that Pythagoras . . . gave was: "Knowledge resides in
numbers that explain Form."[12]

More recently, S. K. Heninger's clear and succinct summaries
offered further clarifications:

[Numbers]
While [Pythagorean metaphysics] posits a dualism, a world of forms
and a world of matter, it nonetheless effectively interrelates them. . . .
[W]hen a mathematician draws a diagram, the figure should be considered conceptual as well as physical. Its ultimate reality still lies in the
intellectual world beyond the senses. [13]

[Cosmos]
The conception of cosmos . . . conveys the notion of *universe* in its literal sense—"all things turning in unison.". . .
    The notion of the cosmos . . . [g]enerally speaking . . . comes down
to two dominant motifs. . . . In one motif cosmos is the reconciliation
of opposites, *concordia discors*. . . . The other motif postulates cosmos
as a unity arising out of a multeity. . . . [T]he two motifs . . . are inter-

related. . . . Cosmos is all-inclusive, exhaustive. It submits to expression by two motifs, however, because either the whole or its parts may be stipulated as its ultimate being. Cosmos comprises both synthesis and analysis.[14]

[The Soul]
Pythagoreans postulated a progress for each soul through a series of incarnations. After the body dies, the individual soul is temporarily assimilated into the world-soul; but soon it is assigned to another body and sent on a journey through another life.[15]

The list of theoretical concerns reads like a guided tour of the issues sounded in all of Aiken's long career: unity in multeity, synthetic and analytic together, the part perceived with the whole. Here indeed is a "crystallization." And yet as Aiken engages in his dialogue over the waves and years with "brother Pythagoras" (SP, 262)—superimposing past and present, New England farmhouse and such ancient landmarks as the Acropolis and Delphi—the reader is aware of a chord struck that makes this late effort singularly satisfying, coming as it does near the end of so complete a career. For though not an autobiographical poem in the sense of being "confessional," "The Crystal" seems one of Aiken's most intimate poems. Not essentially a work of ideas, or one about the "poet" and his aesthetic world and craft, or even a study of a self in relation to family history, "The Crystal" seems to particularize one man's relationship to all of these concerns. Finally, "The Crystal," which is about the possibility of order, the process of knowing, and the importance of attention to poetic skill, is also about the quality of the experience of the individual himself, who "uncovering the miracle of number: all, at last, / transparent, inward and outward" uncovers as well "a pure delight" (SP, 269).

Aiken juggles many balls, dropping none. With his own eyes and with those of Pythagoras, whose story he recalls and whose transmigrating spirit he seems to inherit, he observes the patterns in nature's book—"the law in the wave, and the law in the eye" (SP, 263).

What does not your hand
turn up or over, living or inanimate,
large or small, that does not signal
the miracle of interconnectedness
the beams meeting and crossing in the eye and the mind
as also in the sun? . . .
. . . .
Geometry measures an arc of orchard an arc of sky
the inward march and arch of the mind. Things
are numbers. Numbers are the shape
given to things, immanent in things past and present
as in the things to come.

                                        (SP, 268)

And he makes clear to his readers his conviction that the poem
itself is a way of taking the measure of such a pattern, discerned
by a master pattern perceiver and shaper and linked to the over-
arching patterns of all lived experiences.

                                    So the page turns
always in the middle of a sentence, the beginning of a meaning;
. . . So the prayer, the invocation,
and the revelation, are suspended in our lives,
suspended in a thought.

                                        (SP, 262)

                            All life
is ritual, or becomes so: the elusive pattern
unfolds its arcanum of observances,
measured in time.
                        (SP, 265)

Yet, though the poem ranges far in its somewhat abstract consideration of "numbers, shapes, sounds, measurements, all these
/ to be studied and observed" (SP, 269), we are never very distant
from the tangible frame of reference of one man's particular and
very personal perceptions.

At seven, in the ancient farmhouse,
cocktails sparkle on the tray, the careful answer
succeeds the casual questions, a reasoned dishevelment
ruffling quietly the day's or the hour's issue.
Our names, those we were born with,
or those we were not born with, since all are born
    nameless,
become the material, or the figment, if we wish,
of which to weave, and then unweave, ourselves.
(SP, 264)

The solidity of close detail centers the poem throughout, repeatedly yielding in its immediacy a sense of "joy" and "passion" (SP, 269) in observation and meditation that renders "The Crystal" more than a sparkling web of words and thoughts. The poem, in its intermingling of felt experience and philosophizing, offers a legacy of understanding and affirmation composed by Aiken in the full power of his mature old age, presented to those who will remain behind, having shared in their lifetimes his words, his thoughts, his love, and his love of language.

                  In the ancient farmhouse
which has now become your temple
we listen again to the caucus of robins
the whistle of migrant voices and wings
the turn of the great glass of season.
You taught the migration of souls: all things
must continue, since numbers are deathless:
the mind, like these migrants, crosses all seasons,
and thought, like these cries, is immortal.
The cocktails sparkle, are an oblation.
We pour for the gods, and will always,
you there, we here, and the others who follow,
pour thus in communion. Separate in time,
and yet not separate. Making oblation
in single moment of consciousness
to the endless forever-together.
                  This night
we all set sail for the west.
(SP, 270)

Poetry "is once again staking a claim to its true province," Conrad Aiken remarked in his 1954 acceptance speech for the National Book Award given to *Collected Poems*.[16] This is "nothing less than the kingdom of all knowledge."[17] Throughout a career that spanned more than half of our century, Aiken explored that kingdom with integrity, skill, and feeling. A master of the art of knowing, his work from beginning to end has shown us that

it has always been in poetry, at last, that man has given his thought its supreme expression—which is to say that most of all in poetry he succeeds in making real for himself, and bringing alive, the profound and all but inexplicable myth of existence and experience. In the end, as in the beginning, is the word.[18]

Notes

Notes for Chapter 1: Introduction

1. Aiken's insistence on the importance of form is perhaps most clearly stated in a letter to the poet Ted Berrigan on 28 January 1965: "Letting fly . . . is . . . a dead end street . . . better at your stage to submit yourself doggedly—or even tigerishly—to the hoop of good old Virgilian and Dantean Discipline. . . . [T]here is NOTHING so completely and exclusively fascinating as the *control of form.* And the simultaneous intertwining with it of the Eye—the 'I'—the inner voice, that comes up from undersea" (SL, 318).

2. Here as elsewhere when explaining his creative goals, Aiken echoes the sermons of his grandfather, William James Potter ("I regard myself simply as a continuance of my grandfather" [PR, 120]), and the writing of his most important Harvard teacher, George Santayana ("Santayana's course on the three philosophical poets . . . was one of the best things I ever had anywhere" [Phoenix, 20]). See for example Potter's "The Saving Power of Truth" where he declares, "The truth we want . . . is the absolute and total Reality of things in the universe, whether pertaining to the earth or the heavens, or to matter or thought or spirit, or to any other possibilities of life and existence" (William J. Potter, *Lectures and Sermons,* p. 293). Or note the passage from Santayana's *Three Philosophical Poets,* pp. 13-14, that Aiken quoted many times: "Focus a little experience, give some scope and depth to your feeling, and it grows imaginative; give it more scope and more depth, focus all experience within it . . . and it will grow imaginative in a superlative degree, and be supremely poetical. . . . Poetry, then, is not poetical for being short-winded or incidental, but on the contrary, for being comprehensive and having range." (See Aiken's National Book Award speech, WU, 26 January 1954.)

Notes for Chapter 2: Mixed Modes and Methods

1. Aiken's copy of *Earth Triumphant* is a part of the Huntington Library's Aiken Collection.

2. *Turns and Movies and Other Tales in Verse* (Boston and New York: Houghton Mifflin Company, 1916): *The Jig of Forslin: A Symphony* (Boston: Four Seas Company, 1916); *Nocturne of Remembered Spring and Other Poems* (Boston: Four Seas Company, 1917); *The Charnel Rose; Senlin: A Biography; and Other Poems* (Boston: Four Seas Company, 1918); *Scepticisms* (New York: Alfred A. Knopf, 1919); *The House of Dust: A Symphony* (Boston: Four Seas Company, 1920); *Punch: The Immortal Liar, Documents in His History* (New York: Alfred A. Knopf, 1921); *Priapus and the Pool* (Cambridge, Mass.: Dunster House, 1922); *The Pilgrimage of Festus* (New York: Alfred A. Knopf, 1923);

Bring! Bring! (London: Martin Secker, 1925). I do not include here alternate editions (British or American as the case may be) or regatherings of poems with revisions into new editions.

3. M. L. Rosenthal and Sally M. Gall, *The Modern Poetic Sequence: The Genius of Modern Poetry,* p. 6. This thorough and thoughtful book traces the developments of the modern sequence from its precursors in Shakespeare and Tennyson through contemporary works by Robert Lowell, Austin Clarke, Ted Hughes, and others.

4. Rimbaud's poem reads:

A NOIR, E blanc, I rouge, U vert, O bleu: voyelles,
Je dirai quelque jour vos naissances latentes:
A, noir corset velu des mouches éclatantes
Qui bombinent autour des puanteurs cruelles,

Golfes d'ombre; E, candeurs des vapeurs et des tentes,
Lances des glaciers fiers, rois blancs, frissons d'ombelles;
I, pourpres, sang craché, rire des levres belles
Dans la colère ou les ivresses pénitentes;

U, cycles, vibrements divins des mers virides,
Paix des pâtis semés d'animaux, paix des rides
Que l'alchimie imprime aux grands fronts studieux;

O, supreme Clairon plein de strideurs étranges,
Silences traversés des Mondes et des Anges:
—O l'Oméga, rayon violet de Ses Yeux!
       (Arthur Rimbaud, *Oeuvres Completes,* p. 103)

5. Verlaine's poem reads:

Les sanglots longs
Des violons
    De l'automne
Blessant mon coeur
D'une langueur
    Monotone.

Tout suffocant
Et blême, quand
    Sonne l'heure,
Je me souviens
Des jours anciens
    Et je pleure;

Et je m'en vais
Au vent mauvais
    Qui m'emporte
Deçá, delà,
Pareil à la
    Feuille morte.

(Paul Verlaine, *Oeuvres Poétiques Completes,* pp. 56-57)

For a full discussion of symbolism and the symbolist impact on poetry in English, the reader is urged to read Hugh Kenner's brilliant chapter "Words Set Free," in *The Pound Era.* The focus of my discussion of the poems here, and of the versions of Yeats's "He Remembers Forgotten Beauty," owes a debt to my conversations with Professor Kenner over the past twenty years.

6. See *The Variorum Edition of the Poems of W.B. Yeats,* ed. Peter Allt and Russell K. Alspach, pp. 155-56.

7. See especially the first five of the long poems that Aiken called symphonies and gathered under the title *The Divine Pilgrim:* "The Charnel Rose," written in 1915; "The Jig of Forslin," in 1915-1916; "The House of Dust," in 1916-1917; "Senlin: A Biography," in 1918; and "The Pilgrimage of Festus," in 1919-1920. Typical are the following elusive evocations from "The Charnel Rose," strangely reminiscent of Yeats's "He Remembers Forgotten Beauty":

Her gown was white and lightly blew
A gauze of flame. . . .
Under the singing lamp she stood,
And smiled in subtly fugitive mood,
From depth to depth of wingless skies
Withdrawing batlike down her eyes:
And in his heart an echo came
Of quick dust quaking under flame.
                    (CP, 29)

8. Written by Pound and signed by Flint, the famous statement first appeared in the March 1913 issue of *Poetry.*

9. Ezra Pound, *Gaudier-Brzeska,* p. 92.

10. Responding to Douglas Bridson about whether he "had ever become involved with Imagism," Aiken concluded: "I don't think I ever did affiliate particularly. . . . In fact, I was on the fringes of the various groups. . . . I've met them all, but kept out as much as I could, at the same time frankly trying to pick their brains!" (BBC I, 8). Typical of Aiken's attention to precise renderings of "things" in his early work are lines from "The Jig of Forslin":

And suddenly all the lighted rooms are bare,
. . . .
Men in their shirtsleeves reading papers,
Women by mirrors combing out their hair,
. . . .
And music-filled cafés,
Dancers among white tables slowly turning. . . .
                    (CP, 112)

or from "The House of Dust":

                    the long girder swung
Closer upon him, dropped clanging into place,
. . . Pneumatic hammers
Began their madhouse clatter, the white-hot rivets
Were tossed from below and deftly caught in pails.
                    (CP, 130)

11. Georges Poulet is here describing a portion of Flaubert's *Madame Bovary.* His remark seems to succinctly sum up Aiken's intention and achievement at this stage. See Poulet, *The Metamorphoses of the Circle,* p. 250. I am indebted to Poulet throughout for insights on European literature that relate to my own study of Aiken. On the relationship of subjectivity and objectivity, see too Elisabeth Schneider, *T.S. Eliot: The Pattern in the Carpet,* especially chapters 1–3. I am indebted to Schneider's stimulating observations both in the book and in the many conversations we had about modern writing.

12. Of course the poem was revised after its initial 1918 publication. Because

my intention is to bring the reader to Aiken's work as it is now available, my quotations are not from the original, but from the readily accessible Schocken Books edition of *Selected Poems*.

13. In discussing influences with Douglas Bridson, Aiken observed: "Browning [was] very, very much [an influence]. Just as Pound has confessed I think almost all of us owed a great deal more to Browning than has ever been made apparent. Very curious that: that he shouldn't have credit for restoring the vernacular and coming back to ordinary speech" (BBC II, 2).

14. See Octavio Paz, *The Labyrinth of Solitude: Life and Thought in Mexico*, chapter three, especially pp. 50-52, for a provocative discussion of poetic myth. See too Philip Wheelwright, *The Burning Fountain: A Study in the Language of Symbolism*, particularly chapter 8, "The Mythic Dimension," and Ernst Cassirer, *The Philosophy of Symbolic Forms, Volume Two: Mythical Thought*, especially chapter 1, "The Mythical Consciousness of the Object."

15. Aiken's fascination with the works of Keats and Shelley is well documented throughout his interviews, letters, and essays. The reader who wishes to pursue the connection should look to Aiken's *Collected Criticism*, especially pp. 238-56, and to *Ushant*, especially pp. 143-59.

16. George Santayana, "The Function of Poetry," in *Selected Critical Writings of George Santayana*, ed. Norman Henfrey, 1:72-73.

17. Ralph Waldo Emerson, "History," in *The Works of Ralph Waldo Emerson*, p. 12.

18. See Ralph Waldo Emerson, "The Poet," ibid., pp. 239-66. The importance of Emerson to Aiken is well documented, nowhere so tellingly as in Aiken's "Literature in Massachusetts" (CC, 82-93).

Notes for Chapter 3: Puppets and Showmanship

1. *Preludes for Memnon* (New York and London: Charles Scribner's Sons, 1931); *Time in the Rock: Preludes to Definition* (New York: Charles Scribner's Sons, 1936).

2. Amy Lowell, "Marionettes of Fate," p. 140. See too SL, 59.

3. Charles Dickens, *The Old Curiosity Shop*, p. 132.

4. Ibid., p. 123.

5. See Harry Marten, "Gestural Evil: Techniques of Characterization in Dickens's Early Work," for a full discussion of Dickens's art of "delusion."

6. José Ortega y Gasset, *Meditations on Quixote*, pp. 133-34.

Notes for Chapter 4: Legends, Dreams, and Grotesqueries

1. John Ruskin, "Grotesque Renaissance," in *The Stones of Venice*, 3:126.

2. George Santayana, *The Sense of Beauty*, p. 256.

3. Quoted in William Van O'Connor, *The Grotesque: An American Genre, and Other Essays*, p. 5.

4. Albert Camus, *The Myth of Sisyphus and Other Essays*, p. 6.

5. Wolfgang Kayser, *The Grotesque in Art and Literature*, p. 188.

6. Lee Byron Jennings, *The Ludicrous Demon: Aspects of the Grotesque in German Post-Romantic Prose*, p. 18.

7. See Houston Peterson, *The Melody of Chaos,* p. 205, and BBC I, 14.

8. On page 28 of their *Conrad Aiken: A Bibliography (1902-1978),* Florence and Fraser Bonnell date this early, discarded version of the poem as 1922-1924.

9. As Aiken acknowledged, the poem clearly shares its ideas with *Beyond the Pleasure Principle,* a favorite work; Aiken claims, however, not to have read Freud's work before writing "Deth." See his letter to G. B. Wilbur, 2 January 1931 (SL, 167).

10. A 1962 conversation with Douglas Bridson offers a revealing glimpse of Aiken's fascination with vaudeville:
Aiken: Oh—the Hogarthian quality had a great deal to do with it—but also . . . this was the great age of American slang. The language was proliferating in a fantastic way—both in dialogue and in the words to the songs. It was an extraordinary gold-mine of sheer nomenclature. (BBC I, 4)
See too PR, 116-17.

11. Peterson, *Melody of Chaos,* pp. 205-6. See too the May 1924 letter to Robert Linscott quoted earlier in this text (SL, 92-93).

12. Aiken writes this in a letter quoted in Peterson, *Melody of Chaos,* p. 206.

Notes for Chapter 5: Vaudevillians and Doctors

1. As the Bonnells' *Bibliography* indicates, the 1930 edition of *John Deth: A Metaphysical Legend, and Other Poems* (New York: Charles Scribner's Sons, 1930) includes "Changing Mind, I-IV." *Monthly Criterion* (6 December 1927) contains the work "From Changing Mind,'" reprinted in 1930 as IV of "Changing Mind" in *John Deth.*

2. *Selected Critical Writings of George Santayana,* ed. Norman Henfrey, 1:73.

3. Jonathan Culler, *Structuralist Poetics: Structuralism, Linguistics and the Study of Literature,* p. 135.

4. See Culler, *Structuralist Poetics,* pp. 134-60, for a thorough and thoughtful discussion of the process of "naturalizing" a text.

5. Of course, readers familiar with Aiken's autobiography will recognize and be especially moved by the painful and revealing aspects of the poem as it relates to the poet's own family history. The central fact here is Aiken's discovery at the age of eleven of the bodies of his parents, his mother murdered by his father who then committed suicide. The terrible scene was recalled by Aiken in a 1967 conversation with Joseph Killorin:
And I heard my father's voice counting: "One, two, three." And a pistol shot, and then another shot. I got out of bed and walked through the children's bedroom. . . . I had to step over my father's body to go to my mother. But she was dead, her mouth wide open in the act of screaming. . . . I walked to the police station a block away and told them my father had shot my mother and himself, and they said: "Who is your father?" And I said: "Dr. Aiken." So they came with me and took command. (SL, 4)

6. In his "Note" to "The Coming Forth By Day of Osiris Jones" Aiken is quoting E. A. Wallis Budge's pamphlet entitled *The Book of the Dead* (CP, 1030).

7. E. A. Wallis Budge, *The Book of the Dead: The Papyrus of Ani,* pp. lxix-lxx.

8. Ibid., p. lxx.

9. William Carlos Williams, "Author's Introduction to *The Wedge,*" in *Selected Essays of William Carlos Williams,* p. 256.

10. See *Hamlet* III, iv, 93-95: "Nay, but to live / In the rank sweat of an enseamed bed, / Stew'd in corruption . . ."

11. This is an issue Jonathan Swift explored completely in *Gulliver's Travels.* My point here draws upon Hugh Kenner's chapter "The Gulliver Game," in *The Counterfeiters: An Historical Comedy,* p. 130.

12. See Hugh Kenner, *T.S. Eliot: The Invisible Poet.*

13. Jonathan Holden, *The Rhetoric of the Contemporary Lyric,* p. 117. Although it is a study of contemporary rather than modern poetics, Holden's challenging and illuminating analysis recommends itself to those interested in the full range of modern poetry.

14. Aiken's intense feeling of connection with the methods, goals, and works of Henry James is in evidence throughout *Ushant, Collected Criticism,* and *Selected Letters.* See especially *Collected Criticism,* pp. 230-38, for readings that reveal Aiken's view of James.

Notes for Chapter 6: Absolute Fiction and Beyond

1. See Elisabeth Schneider, *T.S. Eliot: The Pattern in the Carpet,* especially p. 23 and following, for an important discussion of a similar tendency in Eliot's work. Her study of Eliot has influenced mine of Aiken.

2. Percy Shelley, "On Life," in *Shelley's Literary and Philosophical Criticism,* ed. John Shawcross, pp. 54-55. See too Georges Poulet, *The Metamorphoses of the Circle,* p. 102.

3. George Santayana, "The Function of Poetry," in *Selected Critical Writings of George Santayana,* ed. Norman Henfrey, 1:72-73.

4. Readers of the full corpus of Aiken's work will again recognize many of these details. They are drawn from Aiken's own childhood in Savannah and New Bedford and from his own discovery, at the age of eleven and a half, of his father and mother dead after a murder-suicide.

5. My account of the kinds of creative imagining is based upon Philip Wheelwright's categories in his discussions, "Four Ways of Imagination" and "Traits of Expressive Language," in *The Burning Fountain: A Study in the Language of Symbolism.*

6. Samuel Taylor Coleridge, *Biographia Literaria,* chapter 14, in *Coleridge: Selected Poetry and Prose,* ed. Elisabeth Schneider, p. 274. See too Wheelwright, *Burning Fountain,* pp. 45-47.

7. Quoted in Hugh Kenner, *T.S. Eliot: The Invisible Poet,* p. 49.

Notes for Chapter 7: The Circle's Center

1. M. L. Rosenthal and Sally M. Gall, *The Modern Poetic Sequence: The Genius of Modern Poetry,* p. 11.

2. See Ernst Cassirer, *The Philosophy of Symbolic Forms, Volume Two: Mythical Thought,* p. 45, and Philip Wheelwright, *The Burning Fountain: A Study in the Language of Symbolism,* p. 276.

3. Cassirer, *Mythical Thought,* pp. 73-74.

4. Hart Crane, "A Discussion with Hart Crane," *Poetry* 29 (1926): 36.
5. T. E. Hulme, "Notes on Language and Style," *Further Speculations*, p. 87. See Wheelwright, *Burning Fountain*, p. 86.
6. Oskar Seyffert, *Dictionary of Classical Antiquities*, p. 388.
7. Robert Penn Warren, *Brother to Dragons*, pp. 214-15.

Notes for Chapter 8: The Sum of Worlds

1. Wallace Stevens, *Opus Posthumous*, p. 159.
2. Ibid., p. 167.
3. Ibid., p. 158.
4. For a provocative evaluation of poetry's redemptive capacity, see R.W.B. Lewis, *The Poetry of Hart Crane*. Lewis's insights on Crane have marked my reading of Aiken.
5. Homer, *The Odyssey*, in *The Complete Works of Homer*, trans. by S. H. Butcher and Andrew Lang, p. 62. My discussion of the West is indebted to Loren Baritz's excellent article "The Idea of the West."
6. Horace, *Epode 16*, trans. C. J. Kramer, Jr., quoted in Baritz, "Idea of the West," p. 621.
7. For a fascinating discussion of Columbus's journeyings see Henri Baudet, *Paradise on Earth*.
8. Jonathan Edwards, *Thoughts on the Revival of Religion in New England, 1740*, quoted in Baritz, "Idea of the West," p. 637.
9. H. D. Thoreau, "Walking," in *Thoreau: The Major Essays*, ed. J. L. Duncan, p. 204.
10. John Milton, "Paradise Lost," 1:1-6, in *Complete Poems and Major Prose*, ed. Merritt Y. Hughes, p. 211.

Notes for Chapter 9: The Country Clock

1. Jay Martin, *Conrad Aiken: A Life of His Art*, p. 180.
2. A letter of 24 January 1926 to Robert Linscott (WU) suggests that the Blackstone theme had been percolating since at least then. In *Ushant*, Aiken suggests that Blackstone had been "at the back of D's [Aiken's] mind for twenty years" but was "found again and made vivid" when the Massachusetts Guide essay was being researched.
3. "The Kid," *Western Review* 11 (Spring 1947): 133-49.

Notes for Chapter 10: Live for the Borderland

1. Aiken's battle with appalling poverty is clear in various letters, like the one of 19 August 1933 to Robert Linscott: "Just how we continue to live, except that it's almost entirely on borrowed money, and in a perpetual state of torment and anxiety, I find difficult to say" (WU).
2. This tradition is cogently discussed in William C. Spengemann's excellent study *The Adventurous Muse: The Poetics of American Fiction*,

1789-1900. Spengemann's lucid presentation has helped clarify my thinking on the subject.

3. "Bernice" was Bernice Baumgarten, Aiken's agent with Brandt and Brandt.

4. Wallace Stevens, "Connoisseur of Chaos," in *The Collected Poems of Wallace Stevens*, p. 215.

5. Samuel Taylor Coleridge, "Kubla Khan," in *Coleridge: Selected Poetry and Prose*, ed. Elisabeth Schneider, p. 116.

6. See Dwight B. Heath, ed., *A Journal of the Pilgrims at Plymouth: Mourt's Relation*, pp. 15-16. This well-edited and accessible text is recommended to the reader interested in the full narrative.

Notes for Chapter 11: The Unconquerable Ancestors

1. Conrad Aiken, "Poetry and the Mind of Modern Man," in *Poets on Poetry*, ed. Howard Nemerov, p. 2. The essay, published in *Atlantic Monthly* (November 1964), pp. 79-81, was reprinted from the Voice of America Forum Series on American Poetry, coordinated by Howard Nemerov and broadcast by the Voice of America.

2. Of course, these poems were not Aiken's first writings on American themes during the period following his return to America in 1939. In part, the subject of American voices and places had long occupied Aiken. These poems are, however, the major works that most clearly mark the process of Aiken's rediscovery of his ability to "enjoy the American scene whole heartedly again" (U, 135). As listed in the Aiken bibliography prepared by Florence and Fraser Bonnell, a version of "Mayflower" first appeared in *Virginia Quarterly Review* 21 (Spring 1945); "The Kid" appeared in *Western Review* 11 (Spring 1947). *The Kid* appeared as a book in 1947, with notes and corrections. "Mayflower" (slightly revised) and "Hallowe'en" appeared in 1949 in *Skylight One: Fifteen Poems*.

3. Conrad Aiken to Malcolm Lowry, 4 September 1946.

4. Daniel Boorstin, *The Americans: The National Experience*, p. 95.

5. Again Boorstin is helpful, summarizing the nature of life in the borderland: "The pervasive ambiguity of American life, the vagueness which laid the continent open to adventure, which made the land a rich storehouse of the unexpected, which kept vocabulary ungoverned and the language fluid—this same vagueness suffused both the comic and the heroic. Both depended on incongruity: the incongruity of the laughable and the incongruity of the admirable" (ibid., p. 332).

6. Frederick J. Hoffman, *Conrad Aiken*, p. 146.

7. Herman Melville, *Moby-Dick; or, The Whale*, ed. Charles Feidelson, Jr., p. 465.

8. Walt Whitman, *Prose Works 1892, Volume II: Collect and Other Prose*, ed. Floyd Stovall, p. 573.

9. Aiken, "Poetry and the Mind," p. 6.

Notes for Chapter 12: Marriage of Text and Thing

1. Conrad Aiken, "Poetry and the Mind of Modern Man," in *Poets on Poetry*, ed. Howard Nemerov, p. 2.

2. "A Letter from Li Po" was first published in *Chicago Review* 9 (Spring 1955): 74-86. Reprinted in *A Letter From Li Po and Other Poems* (New York: Oxford University Press, 1955), it was revised for *Selected Poems* (New York: Oxford University Press, 1961). "The Crystal" was first published in *Texas Quarterly* 1 (February 1958): 77-86. The poem, with a minor adjustment in word order, was reprinted in *Sheepfold Hill: Fifteen Poems* (New York: Sagamore Press, 1958).

3. As Aiken has said (CP, 1036), Arthur Waley's *The Poetry and Career of Li Po* was a source for his view of Li Po. See page 41 for Waley's discussion of "Hardships of Travel."

4. As Charles Seltman explains in his article "Pythagoras: Artist, Statesman, Philosopher," p. 527, "Although probably over seventy years old, he [Pythagoras] decided to emigrate; and about the year 535 B.C., he left Samos for Italy, never to return." Seltman's article was of great importance to Aiken as a source and stimulus for "The Crystal" (see CP, 1036).

5. Aiken, "Poetry and the Mind," p. 3.

6. William James, *The Pluralistic Universe,* quoted in Peter Goffin, *The Realm of Art,* p. 87.

7. Goffin, *Realm of Art,* pp. 46-47.

8. Ibid., p. 25.

9. Waley, *Career of Li Po,* p. 100.

10. See *The Works of Li Po,* trans. Shigeyashi Obata, pp. 104-6, and Aiken, "A Letter from Li Po," section III (SP, 247-48).

11. Waley, *Career of Li Po,* p. 52.

12. Charles Seltman, "Pythagoras: Artist, Statesman, Philosopher, II. Pythagoras in Italy," p. 596. See Aiken's note of indebtedness (CP, 1036).

13. S. K. Heninger, Jr., *Touches of Sweet Harmony: Pythagorean Cosmology and Renaissance Poetics,* p. 77.

14. Ibid., p. 147.

15. Ibid., p. 267.

16. Conrad Aiken, "Address of Conrad Aiken, National Book Award, New York City, January 26, 1954," p. 2.

17. Ibid., p. 2.

18. Ibid., p. 3.

Selected Aiken Criticism

In 1952 *Wake,* volume 11, edited by Seymour Lawrence, published an important Aiken issue containing essays, letters, and poems by Aiken, Malcolm Cowley, G. Rostrevor Hamilton, Allen Tate, Marianne Moore, Mark Schorer, Marcello Pagnini, Jean Garrigue, Malcolm Lowry, Calvin S. Brown, Henry A. Murray, Julian Symons, and R. W. Stallman. In 1980, *Studies in the Literary Imagination,* volume 13, also published an Aiken issue. Edited by Arthur Waterman and Ted R. Spivey, it contained "a variety of critical perspectives" by its editors, E. P. Bollier, Helen Hagenbuechle, David Mike Hamilton, Catherine Harris, Joseph Killorin, Harry Marten, Douglas Robillard, and Mary Martin Rountree. A Fall 1982 Aiken issue of *Southern Quarterly,* edited by Irving Malin, offered articles by a number of the contributors to the 1980 *Studies in the Literary Imagination* issue, and by Edward Butscher, Irving Malin, Steven Olson, Sanford Pinsker, Nancy Ciucevich Story, Joseph C. Voelker, and James L. Wheeler. These three special issues are illuminating and the reader might want to consult them for a sense of changing responses to Aiken's work. Two valuable books of criticism were published in 1962, and one in 1986: *Conrad Aiken,* by Frederick J. Hoffman (New York: Twayne Publishers, 1962); *Conrad Aiken: A Life of His Art,* by Jay Martin (Princeton, N.J.: Princeton University Press, 1962); and *The Writer as Shaman: The Pilgrimages of Conrad Aiken and Walker Percy,* by Ted R. Spivey (Macon, Ga.: Mercer University Press, 1986).

Since the 1952 issue of *Wake,* several articles on Aiken have appeared. Among the best of these are: Jennifer Aldrich, "The Deciphered Heart," *Sewanee Review* 75 (Summer 1967): 485-520; Rufus A. Blanshard, "Pilgrim's Progress," *Texas Quarterly* 1 (Winter 1958): 135-48; Malcolm Cowley, "Conrad Aiken: From Savannah to Emerson," *Southern Review* 11 (Spring 1975): 245-59; Ted R. Spivey, "Conrad Aiken's 'Ushant': Record of a Contemporary Poet's Quest for Self-Knowledge," *South Atlantic Bulletin* 36 (November 1971): 21-28; and Ted R. Spivey, "Conrad Aiken: Resident of Savannah," *Southern Review* 8 (Autumn 1972): 792-804. My intention in this study has not been to converse with other Aiken critics. But I believe that Aiken has generally been lucky with his critics, and readers of Aiken's works should find these essays thought-provoking.

Bibliography

Works by Conrad Aiken

"Address of Conrad Aiken, National Book Award, New York City, January 26, 1954." TS, Special Collections, Washington University Libraries, St. Louis, Missouri. Published as "The Poets are Awaiting." *Publishers' Weekly* 165 (6 February 1954): 776-77.

And in the Human Heart. New York: Duell, Sloan and Pearce, 1940.

"The Art of Poetry IX, Conrad Aiken: An Interview." Interview by Robert Hunter Wilbur. *Paris Review* 42 (Spring 1968): 97-124.

Blue Voyage. New York: Charles Scribner's Sons, 1927.

Brownstone Eclogues and Other Poems. New York: Duell, Sloan and Pearce, 1942.

The Charnel Rose; Senlin: A Biography; and Other Poems. Boston: Four Seas Company, 1918.

Collected Criticism. London, Oxford, New York: Oxford University Press, 1968.

The Collected Novels of Conrad Aiken. New York, Chicago, San Francisco: Holt, Rinehart and Winston, 1964.

Collected Poems. 2d ed. New York: Oxford University Press, 1970.

The Collected Short Stories of Conrad Aiken. Cleveland and New York: World Publishing Company, 1960.

The Coming Forth by Day of Osiris Jones. New York: Charles Scribner's Sons, 1931.

Conrad Aiken–Robert Linscott Letters. TS, Special Collections, Washington University Libraries, St. Louis, Missouri.

Conversation: or Pilgrims' Progress. New York: Duell, Sloan and Pearce, 1940.

Conversation with Conrad Aiken. BBC Third Programme. Two programs recorded in New York by D. G. Bridson, 11 January 1962 and 18 January 1962. TS, Conrad Aiken Collection, Henry E. Huntington Library, San Marino, California.

The Divine Pilgrim. Athens: University of Georgia Press, 1949.

Great Circle. New York: Charles Scribner's Sons, 1933.

A Heart for the Gods of Mexico. London: Martin Secker, 1939.

The House of Dust: A Symphony. Boston: Four Seas Company, 1920.

"An Interview with Conrad Aiken." Interview by Ashley Brown. *Shenandoah* 15 (Autumn 1963): 18-40.

The Jig of Forslin: A Symphony. Boston: Four Seas Company, 1916.

John Deth: A Metaphysical Legend, and Other Poems. New York: Charles Scribner's Sons, 1930.

The Kid. New York: Duell, Sloan and Pearce, 1947.

King Coffin. New York: Charles Scribner's Sons, 1935.

Landscape West of Eden. London: J. M. Dent & Sons, 1934.

A Letter from Li Po and Other Poems. New York: Oxford University Press, 1955.

The Pilgrimage of Festus. New York: Alfred A. Knopf, 1923.

"Please Continue Mr. Aiken." Interview by Tom Fleming. *Phoenix* (1966), 18-29.

Preludes for Memnon. New York and London: Charles Scribner's Sons, 1931.

Punch: The Immortal Liar, Documents in His History. New York: Alfred A. Knopf, 1921.

Selected Letters of Conrad Aiken. Ed. Joseph Killorin. New Haven and London: Yale University Press, 1978.

Selected Poems. New York: Schocken Books, 1982.

Sheepfold Hill: Fifteen Poems. New York: Sagamore Press, 1958.

Skylight One: Fifteen Poems. New York: Oxford University Press, 1949.

The Soldier: A Poem. Norfolk, Conn.: New Directions, 1944.

Time in the Rock: Preludes to Definition. New York: Charles Scribner's Sons, 1936.

Ushant. New York: Oxford University Press, 1971.

Secondary Works

Aldrich, Jennifer. "The Deciphered Heart." *Sewanee Review* 75 (Summer 1967): 485-520.

Baritz, Loren. "The Idea of the West." *American Historical Review* 66 (April 1961): 618-40.

Baudet, Henri. *Paradise on Earth.* New Haven and London: Yale University Press, 1965.

Blanshard, Rufus A. "Pilgrim's Progress." *Texas Quarterly* 1 (Winter 1958): 135-48.

Boorstin, Daniel. *The Americans: The National Experience.* New York: Vintage Books, 1965.

Budge, E. A. Wallis. *The Book of the Dead: The Papyrus of Ani.* New York: Dover Publications, 1967.

Camus, Albert. *The Myth of Sisyphus and Other Essays.* New York: Alfred A. Knopf, 1975.

Cassirer, Ernst. *The Philosophy of Symbolic Forms, Volume Two: Mythical Thought.* 2 vols. New Haven and London: Yale University Press, 1955.

Coleridge, Samuel Taylor. *Coleridge: Selected Poetry and Prose*. Ed. Elisabeth Schneider. New York: Holt, Rinehart and Winston, 1951.

Cowley, Malcolm. "Conrad Aiken: From Savannah to Emerson." *Southern Review* II (Spring 1975): 245-59.

Culler, Jonathan. *Structuralist Poetics: Structuralism, Linguistics and the Study of Literature*. Ithaca: Cornell University Press, 1975.

Dickens, Charles. *The Old Curiosity Shop*. London: Oxford University Press, 1951.

Emerson, Ralph Waldo. *The Works of Ralph Waldo Emerson*. New York: Tudor Publishing Company, n.d.

Goffin, Peter. *The Realm of Art*. London: Lindsay Drummond, 1946.

Heath, Dwight B., ed. *A Journal of the Pilgrims at Plymouth: Mourt's Relation*. New York: Corinth Books, 1963.

Heninger, S. K., Jr. *Touches of Sweet Harmony: Pythagorean Cosmology and Renaissance Poetics*. San Marino, Calif.: Huntington Library, 1974.

Hoffman, Frederick J. *Conrad Aiken*. New York: Twayne Publishers, 1962.

Holden, Jonathan. *The Rhetoric of the Contemporary Lyric*. Bloomington: Indiana University Press, 1980.

Homer. *The Odyssey*. In *The Complete Works of Homer*. Trans. S. H. Butcher and Andrew Lang. New York: Modern Library, n.d.

Hulme, T. E. *Further Speculations*. Minneapolis: University of Minnesota Press, 1955.

Jennings, Lee Byron. *The Ludicrous Demon: Aspects of the Grotesque in German Post-Romantic Prose*. Publications in Modern Philology, vol. 70. Berkeley and Los Angeles: University of California Press, 1963.

Kayser, Wolfgang. *The Grotesque in Art and Literature*. New York and Toronto: McGraw Hill, 1963.

Kenner, Hugh. *The Counterfeiters; An Historical Comedy*. Bloomington: Indiana University Press, 1968.

———. *The Pound Era*. Berkeley and Los Angeles: University of California Press, 1971.

———. *T.S. Eliot: The Invisible Poet*. New York: Citadel Press, 1964.

Lawrence, Seymour, ed. Conrad Aiken Number, *Wake* II (1952).

Lewis, R.W.B. *The Poetry of Hart Crane*. Princeton, N.J.: Princeton University Press, 1967.

Li, Po. *The Works of Li Po*. Trans. Shigeyoshi Obata. New York: E. P. Dutton, 1922.

Lowell, Amy. "Marionettes of Fate." *New Republic* 28 (September 1921): 139-40.

Malin, Irving, ed. Aiken issue, *Southern Quarterly* 21 (Fall 1982).

Marten, Harry. "Conrad Aiken's 'Absolute Fiction': *Blue Voyage* and *Great Circle*." *ELH* 45 (1978): 325-42.

――――. "Gestural Evil: Techniques of Characterization in Dickens' Early Work." *Ball State University Forum* 17 (Autumn 1976): 20-27.

――――. "'The Stranger Becomes Oneself': Visual Surfaces and Patterns in Conrad Aiken's *King Coffin.*" *Journal of Narrative Technique* 9 (Winter 1979): 33-40.

――――. "The Unconquerable Ancestors: 'Mayflower,' 'The Kid,' 'Hallowe'en.'" *Studies in the Literary Imagination* 13 (Fall 1980): 51-62.

Martin, Jay. *Conrad Aiken: A Life of His Art.* Princeton, N.J.: Princeton University Press, 1962.

Melville, Herman. *Moby-Dick; or, The Whale.* Ed. Charles Feidelson, Jr. Indianapolis, Ind.: Bobbs-Merrill, Co., 1964.

Milton, John. *Complete Poems and Major Prose.* Ed. Merritt Y. Hughes. New York: Odyssey Press, 1957.

Nemerov, Howard, ed. *Poets on Poetry.* New York: Basic Books, 1966.

O'Connor, William Van. *The Grotesque: An American Genre, and Other Essays.* Carbondale: Southern Illinois University Press, 1962.

Ortega y Gasset, José. *Meditations on Quixote.* New York: W. W. Norton & Company, 1961.

Paz, Octavio. *The Labyrinth of Solitude: Life and Thought in Mexico.* New York: Grove Press, 1961.

Peterson, Houston. *The Melody of Chaos.* New York and Toronto: Longmans, Green and Co., 1931.

Potter, William J. *Lectures and Sermons.* Boston: Geo. H. Ellis, 1895.

Poulet, Georges. *The Metamorphoses of the Circle.* Baltimore: Johns Hopkins Press, 1966.

Pound, Ezra. *Gaudier-Brzeska.* New York: New Directions, 1960.

Rimbaud, Arthur. *Oeuvres Completes.* Paris: Gallimard, 1963.

Rosenthal, M. L., and Sally M. Gall. *The Modern Poetic Sequence: The Genius of Modern Poetry.* New York and Oxford: Oxford University Press, 1983.

Ruskin, John. *The Stones of Venice.* 3 vols. New York: John Wiley and Sons, 1884.

Santayana, George. *Selected Critical Writings of George Santayana.* 2 vols. Ed. Norman Henfrey. London and New York: Cambridge University Press, 1968.

――――. *The Sense of Beauty.* New York: Charles Scribner's Sons, 1904.

――――. *Three Philosophical Poets.* Cambridge: Harvard University Press, 1910, 1935.

Schneider, Elisabeth. *T.S. Eliot: The Pattern in the Carpet.* Berkeley, Los Angeles, London: University of California Press, 1975.

Seltman, Charles. "Pythagoras: Artist, Statesman, Philosopher." *History Today* 6 (August 1956): 522-28.

――――. "Pythagoras: Artist, Statesman, Philosopher II. Pythagoras in Italy." *History Today* 6 (September 1956): 592-98.

Seyffert, Oskar. *Dictionary of Classical Antiquities*. Rev. ed. Ed. Henry Nettleship and J. E. Sandys. Cleveland and New York: World Publishing Company, 1956.

Shakespeare, William. *The Riverside Shakespeare*. Boston: Houghton Mifflin Company, 1974.

Shelley, Percy. *Shelley's Literary and Philosophical Criticism*. Ed. John Shawcross. London: Oxford University Press, 1932.

Spengemann, William C. *The Adventurous Muse: The Poetics of American Fiction, 1789-1900*. New Haven and London: Yale University Press, 1977.

Spivey, Ted R. "Conrad Aiken: Resident of Savannah." *Southern Review* 8 (Autumn 1972): 792-804.

————. "Conrad Aiken's 'Ushant': Record of a Contemporary Poet's Quest for Self-Knowledge." *South Atlantic Bulletin* 36 (November 1971): 21-28.

————. *The Writer as Shaman: The Pilgrimages of Conrad Aiken and Walker Percy*. Macon, Ga.: Mercer University Press, 1986.

Stevens, Wallace. *The Collected Poems of Wallace Stevens*. New York: Alfred A. Knopf, 1968.

————. *Opus Posthumous*. New York: Alfred A. Knopf, 1971.

Thoreau, H. D. *Thoreau: The Major Essays*. Ed. J. L. Duncan. New York: Dutton, 1972.

Verlaine, Paul. *Oeuvres Poétiques Completes*. Paris: Gallimard, 1948.

Waley, Arthur. *The Poetry and Career of Li Po*. London: George Allen and Unwin, 1950.

Warren, Robert Penn. *Brother to Dragons*. New York: Random House, 1953.

Waterman, Arthur, and Ted R. Spivey, eds. *Conrad Aiken. Studies in the Literary Imagination* 13 (Fall 1980).

Wheelwright, Philip. *The Burning Fountain: A Study in the Language of Symbolism*. Bloomington and London: Indiana University Press, 1968.

Whitman, Walt. *Prose Works 1892, Volume II: Collect and Other Prose*. Ed. Floyd Stovall. New York: New York University Press, 1964.

Williams, William Carlos. *Selected Essays of William Carlos Williams*. New York: Random House, 1954.

Yeats, W. B. *The Variorum Edition of the Poems of W.B. Yeats*. Ed. Peter Allt and Russell K. Alspach. New York: Macmillan Co., 1957.

For a complete bibliography of works by Conrad Aiken see F. W. and F. C. Bonnell, comps., *Conrad Aiken: A Bibliography (1902-1978)* (San Marino, Calif.: Huntington Library, 1982).

Name and Subject Index

Index to Quotations from Aiken's Works

Permissions

Portions of chapters 6 and II first appeared in "Conrad Aiken's 'Absolute Fiction': *Blue Voyage* and *Great Circle,*" *ELH* 45 (1978): 325-42, reprinted by permission of the Johns Hopkins University Press; "'The Stranger Becomes Oneself': Visual Surfaces and Patterns in Conrad Aiken's *King Coffin,*" *Journal of Narrative Technique* 9 (Winter 1979): 33-40, reprinted by permission of the editors; and "The Unconquerable Ancestors: 'Mayflower,' 'The Kid,' 'Halowe'en,'" *Studies in the Literary Imagination* 13 (Fall 1980): 51-62, reprinted by permission of the editors.

Selections from *Collected Criticism* by Conrad Aiken, Oxford University Press, copyright © 1935, 1939, 1940, 1942, 1951, 1958 by Conrad Aiken, copyright renewed 1963, 1967, 1968, 1970, 1971 by Conrad Aiken, copyright renewed 1986 by Mary H. Aiken, reprinted by permission of Brandt & Brandt Literary Agents.

Selections from *Collected Poems* by Conrad Aiken, copyright © 1953 by Conrad Aiken, reprinted by permission of Oxford University Press.

Lines from "Knowing" by Conrad Aiken, 1974, reprinted by permission of the Huntington Library, San Marino, California.

Selections from *Selected Letters of Conrad Aiken* edited by Joseph Killorin, copyright © 1978 by Mary Hoover Aiken and Joseph I. Killorin, reprinted by permission of Yale University Press.

Selections from *Selected Poems* by Conrad Aiken, copyright © 1961 by Conrad Aiken, reprinted by permission of Oxford University Press. Selections from *Ushant* by Conrad Aiken, copyright © 1971 by Conrad Aiken, reprinted by permission of Oxford University Press.

Excerpts of selected letters from the Aiken Collection, Huntington Library, San Marino, California, reprinted by permission of the Huntington Library.

Excerpts of selected Conrad Aiken-Robert Linscott letters from the Conrad Aiken Papers, Special Collections, Washington University Libraries, St. Louis, Missouri, reprinted by permission of the Washington University Libraries. Selections from "Conversations with Conrad Aiken" recorded by Douglas G. Bridson, 1962, reprinted by permission of the Huntington Library, San Marino, California.